Copyright 2023 Anna J Parkerson

Table of Contents

Introduction

- Why YouTube?
- Who This Book Is For

Chapter 1: Getting Started

- 1.1 Setting Up Your YouTube Channel
- 1.2 Choosing Your Niche
- 1.3 Understanding YouTube's Policies

Chapter 2: Creating Your First Video

- 2.1 Planning Your Content
- 2.2 Shooting Your Video
- 2.3 Editing and Uploading

Chapter 3: Growing Your Channel

- 3.1 Understanding YouTube Analytics
- 3.2 Promoting Your Videos
- 3.3 Collaborating with Other YouTubers

Chapter 4: Building Your Audience

- 4.1 Engaging with Your Viewers
- 4.2 Building a Community
- 4.3 Audience Retention Strategies

Chapter 5: Monetization

- 5.1 Ad Revenue and Partner Programs
- 5.2 Sponsored Content
- 5.3 Merchandise and Affiliate Marketing

Chapter 6: Legal and Copyright Considerations

- 6.1 Copyright Issues
- 6.2 Fair Use and Creative Commons
- 6.3 Protecting Your Content

Chapter 7: Advanced Tips and Tricks

- 7.1 SEO and Video Optimization
- 7.2 Livestreaming and Premieres
- 7.3 YouTube Algorithm Insights

Chapter 8: Case Studies

- 8.1 Successful YouTubers' Journeys
- 8.2 Lessons from Real-Life Examples
- 8.3 Finding Your Unique Path

Chapter 9: Troubleshooting and FAQ

- 9.1 Common Problems and Solutions
- 9.2 Frequently Asked Questions

Chapter 10: Beyond YouTube

Introduction

Why YouTube?

1.   **Global Reach:** YouTube is one of the largest and most visited websites on the internet, with over 2 billion logged-in monthly users as of my knowledge cutoff date in January 2022. It is accessible to people all over the world, making it a powerful platform for sharing your content with a global audience. If you want to reach a wide and diverse viewership, YouTube is an ideal place to do so.

2.   **Diverse Content:** YouTube hosts an incredibly diverse range of content. From educational tutorials and entertainment to vlogs and product reviews, there's something for everyone. This variety allows content creators to find their niche and cater to a specific audience, no matter how niche their interests may be.

3.   **Search Engine Visibility:** YouTube is the second largest search engine after Google, which is particularly advantageous for content creators. When people are looking for information, how-to guides, or answers to their questions, they often turn to YouTube. Optimizing your content for search can help you attract a significant viewership.

4. **Monetization Opportunities:** YouTube offers several ways to make money from your content. You can earn revenue through ads, channel memberships, merchandise shelf integration, and more. This can make YouTube a source of income for creators who build a substantial audience.

5. **Community Building:** YouTube allows for direct interaction with your audience. Creators can engage with their viewers through comments, live chats, and community posts. Building a loyal fan base and a sense of community around your content is a powerful way to grow your channel.

6. **Educational Resources:** Many beginners turn to YouTube to learn about a wide range of topics. As a content creator, you can share your expertise and knowledge with others, positioning yourself as an authority in your niche.

7. **Creative Outlet:** For those with a passion for filmmaking, storytelling, or any form of visual and audio expression, YouTube provides a platform to showcase your creativity. You have the freedom to experiment with different content styles and formats, fostering your creative skills.

8. **Career Opportunities:** Success on YouTube can lead to various career opportunities, including partnerships, sponsorships, speaking engagements, and book deals. It can also be a

stepping stone to other forms of media and entertainment.

9. **Flexibility and Convenience:** YouTube's platform is user-friendly, and you can create content with minimal equipment. This makes it accessible to beginners with limited resources. You can upload videos on your schedule, providing a level of flexibility that other media outlets may not offer.

10. **Long-Term Potential:** YouTube content has the potential to generate passive income over the long term. Once you've created and uploaded a video, it can continue to attract views and generate revenue for years to come.

While YouTube offers numerous benefits, it's important to note that building a successful channel takes time, effort, and dedication. Consistency and quality content are key factors in attracting and retaining viewers. Additionally, staying informed about YouTube's policies and best practices is essential for long-term success on the platform.

Who This Book Is For

The book "YouTube Secrets for Beginners" is primarily targeted at individuals who are new to the world of YouTube and are looking to start their journey as content creators. It aims to provide essential guidance, insights, and strategies to help beginners navigate the platform effectively. Here's a detailed breakdown of the intended audience for this book:

1.   **Aspiring YouTubers:** This book is specifically designed for those who have a desire to become YouTubers but lack the knowledge and experience to get started. It provides a step-by-step roadmap for building and growing a YouTube channel from scratch.

2.   **Content Creators:** Whether you want to create vlogs, tutorials, product reviews, or any other form of content, this book is suitable for individuals who are passionate about creating and sharing their ideas, knowledge, and experiences with a broader online audience.

3.   **Small Business Owners:** Entrepreneurs and small business owners looking to harness the power of YouTube for marketing, branding, and reaching a wider customer base will find valuable tips and

techniques to promote their products or services effectively.

4. **Students and Educators:** Students, teachers, and educators interested in using YouTube as an educational platform will learn how to create and manage educational content, engage with students, and create a digital learning community.

5. **Parents and Guardians:** Parents or guardians who want to understand YouTube and its safety features to ensure a safe online experience for their children will find this book useful. It covers parental controls, privacy settings, and content filtering.

6. **Marketing and PR Professionals:** Beginners in the field of marketing, public relations, and social media will benefit from the insights on how to use YouTube as a marketing tool. This includes strategies for creating engaging content and effectively reaching a target audience.

7. **Nonprofit Organizations:** This book is also suitable for nonprofits and charitable organizations looking to use YouTube to raise awareness for their causes, engage with potential supporters, and create a social impact.

8. **Technically Challenged Individuals:** Beginners who may not be tech-savvy will

appreciate the straightforward and user-friendly explanations provided in the book, making the process of starting a YouTube channel less intimidating.

9. **Seniors and Retirees:** Older individuals looking to share their wisdom, experiences, or hobbies with a broader audience can learn how to use YouTube as a platform to connect with like-minded individuals and potentially monetize their content.

10. **Creative Hobbyists:** Artists, musicians, crafters, and individuals with creative hobbies who want to showcase their work or talent on YouTube will find guidance on how to create engaging content, gain visibility, and connect with their creative communities.

11. **Cultural and Niche Enthusiasts:** Those passionate about specific cultures, traditions, or niche interests can learn how to use YouTube to connect with a global audience who shares their interests.

12. **Community Builders:** Aspiring community builders who want to create, nurture, and grow a community around their content or interests can benefit from the book's advice on building an engaged audience.

In essence, "YouTube Secrets for Beginners" is intended for anyone who wants to learn how to navigate YouTube effectively, create engaging content, build an audience, and potentially turn their passion into a sustainable online presence. It provides the foundational knowledge required to take the first steps on the platform, regardless of the specific goals or interests of the reader

Chapter 1: Getting Started

1.1 Setting Up Your YouTube Channel

Setting up your YouTube channel is the first crucial step in your journey as a content creator on the platform. This section of the book will provide a detailed guide on how to establish your YouTube presence effectively. Here's a breakdown of what you can expect to learn in this chapter:

1.   **Creating Your YouTube Account:**

•   **Email Address:** You'll learn how to use or create a Google account, as YouTube is owned by Google. If you already have a Google account, this step is simplified.

•   **YouTube Channel Name:** Choosing a memorable and relevant channel name is vital. The book will guide you on selecting a name that represents your content and aligns with your niche.

2.   **Customizing Your Channel:**

•   **Profile Picture:** You'll discover the importance of choosing a recognizable profile picture, such as a logo or a clear image of yourself.

- **Channel Art:** Learn how to create an engaging banner image that visually represents your channel and appeals to potential subscribers.

- **About Section:** Understand how to craft a compelling "About" section that describes your channel's content and encourages viewers to subscribe.

3. **Channel Settings:**

- **Privacy Settings:** Explore the various privacy settings for your channel, including public, unlisted, and private video options, and learn how to choose the most suitable settings for your content.

- **Advanced Settings:** Discover additional settings, such as allowing comments, setting up a custom URL, and linking your social media accounts to your channel.

4. **Uploading Your First Video:**

- **Understanding Video Formats:** Learn about the video formats and recommended settings for your content.

- **Uploading and Publishing:** Get step-by-step instructions on uploading your first video, including selecting a video title, description, tags, and thumbnail.

5. Branding Your Channel:

• **Creating a Channel Trailer:** Understand how to create a channel trailer video that introduces new visitors to your content and encourages them to subscribe.

• **Organizing Your Content:** Learn how to create playlists and categories to make it easier for viewers to navigate your channel and discover related videos.

6. Channel Optimization:

• **Channel Keywords:** Discover how to choose and optimize keywords for your channel to improve its discoverability on YouTube and search engines.

• **Setting up a Posting Schedule:** Understand the importance of consistency and learn how to create and adhere to a posting schedule that suits your content production capabilities.

7. Engaging with Your Audience:

• **Enabling Notifications:** Learn how to encourage viewers to enable notifications for your channel so they are alerted when you post new content.

• **Interacting with Comments:** Understand the significance of engaging with comments and learn how to foster a sense of community around your channel.

8. Setting Your Channel Branding and Layout:

•   **Channel Icon and Banner:** Explore how to update and maintain your channel icon and banner as your content evolves.

•   **Arranging Your Sections:** Learn how to customize your channel's layout, such as arranging featured videos, playlists, and popular uploads.

9.   Understanding the YouTube Studio::

•   **Navigating YouTube Studio:** Get acquainted with the YouTube Studio dashboard, where you can manage your videos, audience analytics, and channel settings.

1.2 Choosing Your Niche

Selecting the right niche is a critical decision when you're starting your YouTube journey. Your niche is the topic or subject matter that your YouTube channel will primarily focus on.

1.   Understanding the Importance of a Niche:

A niche allows you to target a specific audience interested in your content, helping you stand out in a crowded platform like YouTube.

2.   Self-Assessment:

Identifying Your Passions: The first step is to evaluate your interests and passions. What do you love to talk about, learn, or create content around? Identifying these interests is a crucial starting point.

3.   Market Research:

Identifying Demand: You'll learn how to research the YouTube platform to determine which niches are currently popular and have a significant audience. Analyzing trends and audience demand is key.

4.   Competition Analysis:

Evaluating Competing Channels: Understanding your competition is crucial. You'll learn how to assess existing YouTube channels in your chosen niche, identify gaps or opportunities, and decide how you can differentiate yourself.

5.   Niche Size and Viability:

Assessing Audience Size: Discover how to estimate the size of the potential audience for your chosen niche. This can help you determine whether your niche has enough viewers to support your channel.

6. **Passion vs. Profit:**

Balancing Interests and Market Potential: You'll explore how to strike a balance between your interests and the profit potential of a niche.

7. **Unique Value Proposition:**

Defining Your Unique Angle: You'll learn how to identify and articulate your unique value proposition. This is what sets your channel apart and gives viewers a compelling reason to subscribe.

8. **Content Ideas and Consistency:**

Developing Content Ideas: Understand how to brainstorm content ideas within your niche.

9. **Flexibility and Adaptability:**

Evaluating Long-Term Viability: Assess how your chosen niche can evolve over time.

10. **Ethical Considerations:**

Exploring Ethical Boundaries: You'll gain insights into ethical considerations within your niche and understand how to create content that aligns with your values and maintains your integrity.

11. **Finalizing Your Niche:**

Making a Decision: After conducting thorough research and self-assessment, you'll be guided through the process of finalizing your niche and making a commitment to your chosen content area.

12.   Pivoting and Experimentation:

This book will cover the concept of pivoting or experimenting with your niche if you find that your initial choice doesn't yield the expected results. It's essential to remain open to adjustments as you gain experience on YouTube.

1.3 Understanding YouTube's Policies

Before diving headfirst into content creation on YouTube, it's crucial to understand the platform's policies and guidelines. This section of the book will provide you with a detailed understanding of YouTube's policies, rules, and best practices. Here's a comprehensive breakdown of what you can expect to learn:

1.   Community Guidelines:

Content Policies: Gain insight into YouTube's community guidelines, which outline what is and isn't allowed on the platform. This includes policies on hate speech, harassment, violence, and other prohibited content.

- **Strikes and Penalties:** Understand how YouTube enforces its community guidelines, including the concept of strikes and the potential penalties for violating these rules.

2. **Copyright and Fair Use:**

- **Copyright Basics:** Learn about copyright law as it pertains to YouTube, including what constitutes copyrighted material and how to respect the rights of content creators.

- **Fair Use:** Understand the concept of fair use and how it can be applied when using copyrighted material in your content while staying within legal boundaries.

3. **Monetization Policies:**

- **Ad Revenue Eligibility:** Explore the requirements and policies for earning revenue through YouTube's Partner Program, including subscriber and watch time thresholds.

- **Ad Placement and Types:** Understand how ads are placed on your videos, the different types of ads (e.g., skippable, non-skippable), and ad-friendly content guidelines.

4. **Data and Privacy:**

- **User Privacy:** Learn how YouTube handles user data and the importance of respecting viewer privacy, especially in the context of regulations like GDPR and COPPA.

- **Child-Directed Content:** Understand the guidelines for creating content intended for children and the associated privacy considerations.

5. **Community Engagement:**

- **Comment and Interaction Policies:** Explore YouTube's policies regarding comments, including spam and inappropriate behavior, and learn how to moderate and engage with your audience effectively.

- **Sub4Sub and Engagement Bait:** Understand the platform's stance on "sub4sub" and engagement bait tactics and why it's important to avoid them.

6. **Monetization and Partner Program:**

- **Eligibility and Requirements:** Delve into the requirements for joining the YouTube Partner Program, including subscriber and watch hour thresholds.

- **Monetization Strategies:** Learn about monetization options on YouTube, such as ad revenue, channel memberships, merchandise shelf, and Super Chat.

7. Ad Policies:

- **Ad Placement and Content:** Understand where ads can appear on your videos and the type of content that is eligible for monetization.

- **Ad Revenue Sharing:** Learn about revenue sharing between YouTubers and the platform and how to maximize your ad revenue potential.

8. Channel Policies:

- **Channel Suspension and Termination:** Understand the reasons a channel can be suspended or terminated, including multiple community guideline violations and copyright strikes.

- **Account Recovery:** Learn about the steps to take in case your account is wrongly suspended and how to request a review.

9. Content Creation and Strategies:

- **Best Practices:** Discover best practices for creating content that complies with YouTube's policies while maximizing your viewership and engagement.

- **Content Warnings and Age Restrictions:** Learn how to apply content warnings and age restrictions to your videos when necessary.

10. **Updates and Resources:**

- **Staying Informed:** Explore how to stay up-to-date with YouTube's policies and any changes or updates to the platform's guidelines.

- **YouTube Help Center:** Understand how to use the YouTube Help Center as a valuable resource for addressing policy-related questions and issues.

11. **Appeals and Disputes:**

- **Appealing Strikes and Claims:** Learn how to appeal copyright strikes, content ID claims, or other policy violations and the steps involved in the appeals process.

Understanding YouTube's policies is essential for ensuring a smooth and compliant journey on the platform.

Chapter 2: Creating Your First Video

2.1 Planning Your Content

Creating engaging and well-structured content is at the heart of a successful YouTube channel. This section of the book will guide you through the process of planning your content effectively

Understanding Your Audience:

• **Audience Demographics:** You'll learn how to identify your target audience's age, gender, location, interests, and preferences. Understanding your viewers is key to creating content that resonates with them.

2. **Defining Your Content Goals:**

• **Educational, Entertainment, or Informative:** Explore different content categories, such as educational, entertainment, or informative content, and determine which aligns best with your channel's purpose.

• **Value Proposition:** Define the unique value you intend to offer to your viewers. What problem will your content solve, or what entertainment or information will it provide?

3. **Content Research:**

- **Trending Topics:** Discover how to research trending topics and popular content within your niche. Tools and strategies for staying updated will be covered.

- **Keyword Research:** Understand how to conduct keyword research to optimize your content for search engines and YouTube's recommendation system.

4. **Video Format and Style:**

- **Choosing Video Formats:** Learn about various video formats, such as tutorials, vlogs, reviews, and more, and select the format that aligns with your content goals and audience preferences.

- **Developing a Style:** Explore how to define your content's style, including your on-camera presence, tone, and branding.

5. **Scripting and Storyboarding:**

- **Content Structure:** Understand how to create a content structure that keeps your viewers engaged, such as introductions, hooks, and clear, informative content.

- **Scripting Techniques:** Learn how to write scripts, or outlines, for your videos. Effective scripting can help you stay on track and ensure your message is clear.

6.   Video Planning:

•   **Equipment and Setup:** Explore the basics of the equipment you'll need, such as cameras, microphones, lighting, and video editing software.

•   **Location and Set Design:** Discover how to set up your recording space for optimal video and audio quality. This includes background, props, and visual branding elements.

7.   Content Calendar:

•   **Scheduling and Consistency:** Develop a content calendar that outlines your video release schedule. Maintaining and expanding your following requires consistency. Consistency is key to retaining and growing your audience.

•   **Balancing Evergreen and Trending Content:** Understand how to balance between evergreen content (timeless content) and trending or topical content to maintain a diverse and engaging channel.

8.   Optimizing for Audience Retention:

•   **Engagement Techniques:** Learn how to keep your viewers watching by using engagement techniques like storytelling, questions, and interactive elements.

• **Video Length and Watch Time:** Understand how video length can impact audience retention and learn strategies to optimize your videos for longer watch times.

9. **SEO and Metadata:**

• **Title and Description:** Discover how to craft compelling video titles and descriptions that attract viewers and improve discoverability.

• **Tags and Thumbnails:** Learn how to use tags and create eye-catching thumbnails that encourage clicks and views.

10. **Branding and Visual Identity:**

• **Channel Branding:** Explore how to establish a consistent visual identity for your channel through branding elements like logos, colors, and visual motifs.

• **Thumbnail Design:** Understand the importance of creating visually appealing and click-worthy thumbnails for your videos.

11. **Collaborations and Promotion:**

- **Collaborative Opportunities:** Learn how to identify collaboration opportunities with other content creators and influencers.

- **Promotion Strategies:** Explore techniques for promoting your videos on social media, forums, and other online communities.

12. **Feedback and Adaptation:**

- **Audience Feedback:** Understand the significance of audience feedback and how to use it to improve your content.

- **Adapting to Trends:** Learn how to adapt your content strategy to changing trends and audience interests.

Planning your content is a foundational step in your YouTube journey.

2.2 Shooting Your Video

Shooting your video is the phase where your content comes to life. It's essential to capture high-quality footage and audio while maintaining a captivating on-screen presence. Let's explore the details of shooting your video for your YouTube channel:

1. **Camera and Equipment:**

- **Selecting the Right Camera:** Understand the different types of cameras suitable for YouTube, from smartphones to DSLRs, and choose the one that aligns with your needs and budget.

- **Tripods and Stabilization:** Learn about the importance of stable shots and how tripods, gimbals, and other stabilization tools can improve the quality of your videos.

2. **Lighting Setup:**

- **Natural vs. Artificial Light:** Explore the pros and cons of using natural light versus artificial lighting sources, and how to set up your lighting for the best results.

- **Three-Point Lighting:** Learn the basics of three-point lighting, which includes the key light, fill light, and backlight, to achieve professional and flattering lighting for your videos.

3. **Sound Recording:**

- **Microphones:** Understand the different microphone options, including lavalier, shotgun, and USB microphones, and select the one that suits your recording environment and needs.

- **Audio Setup:** Learn how to set up your microphone for optimal sound quality, including minimizing background noise and echoes.

4. Framing and Composition:

• **Camera Angles and Framing:** Explore camera angles such as wide, medium, and close-up shots, as well as framing techniques like the rule of thirds to make your videos visually appealing.

• **Rule of Focus:** Understand how to use focus to draw your viewers' attention to the most critical elements in your shots.

5. Camera Settings:

• **Resolution and Frame Rate:** Learn how to choose the right resolution (e.g., 1080p, 4K) and frame rate for your videos, considering the look and feel you want to achieve.

• **Exposure and White Balance:** Understand exposure settings, such as aperture, shutter speed, and ISO, and how to set the correct white balance for accurate colors.

6. Recording Techniques:

• **Multiple Takes:** Discover the benefits of shooting multiple takes to ensure you have a variety of shots and angles to choose from in the editing process.

• **B-Roll and Cutaways:** Learn how to capture additional footage, known as B-roll, to enhance your videos and maintain viewer engagement.

7. **On-Camera Performance:**

• **Confidence and Presence:** Understand the importance of confidence and on-screen presence. Tips for maintaining a strong and engaging presence on camera will be covered.

• **Script Delivery:** If you're following a script, learn techniques for natural and engaging script delivery, including managing pacing and intonation.

8. **Continuity and Editing Considerations:**

• **Consistency:** Explore strategies for maintaining visual and audio consistency in your shots, even when filming on different days.

• **Editing Planning:** Consider how your video will be edited and plan your shooting accordingly, including capturing specific shots for transitions or overlays.

9. **Camera Movement:**

• **Static vs. Dynamic Shots:** Understand the impact of camera movement and when it's appropriate to use static shots or dynamic camera movements like pans, tilts, or tracking shots.

10. Recording Best Practices:

• **Recording Environment:** Learn how to create a controlled recording environment, including minimizing external noise and distractions.

• **Backup and Redundancy:** Understand the importance of backup solutions for your video and audio recordings to avoid data loss.

11. Review and Feedback:

• **Self-Review:** Discover how to review your footage and make improvements during the shooting process.

• **Seeking Feedback:** Learn the benefits of seeking feedback from others to enhance the quality of your content.

2.3 Editing and Uploading

Editing and uploading your video is a crucial phase in the content creation process. It involves transforming your raw footage into a polished and engaging video that is ready to be shared with your audience on YouTube.

Video Editing Software:

• **Choosing Editing Software:** Understand the various video editing software options available, both free and paid, and select the one that best suits your needs and skill level.

• **Basic Editing Tools:** Learn about the essential tools and features in video editing software, such as cutting, trimming, transitions, and effects.

2. **Importing and Organizing Footage:**

• **Importing Files:** Discover how to import your video and audio files into the editing software.

• **Organizing Footage:** Learn how to create a structured system for managing your clips, audio tracks, and other media assets.

3. **Timeline and Sequencing:**

• **Timeline Layout:** Understand the timeline layout in your editing software and how to organize your clips to create a coherent story or presentation.

• **Sequencing and Arrangement:** Explore techniques for arranging your clips in a logical order to maintain viewer engagement.

4.   Cutting and Trimming:

•   **Basic Cutting:** Learn how to trim and cut clips to remove unwanted footage and maintain a cohesive narrative.

•   **Precision Editing:** Discover tips for precise trimming, splitting, and arranging clips to align with your script or story.

5.   Transitions and Effects:

•   **Transition   Types:** Understand different types of transitions, such as cuts, fades, wipes, and more, and how to apply them for smooth scene changes.

•   **Visual Effects:** Explore how to add visual effects, color correction, and filters to enhance the visual quality of your video.

6.   Audio Editing:

•   **Audio Enhancement:** Learn how to edit audio tracks, including adjusting volume, removing background noise, and adding music or sound effects.

•   **Voiceovers:** Discover how to record and incorporate voiceovers into your video to provide narration or commentary.

7.   Text and Graphics:

- **Adding Titles and Text:** Understand how to include text, titles, and captions in your video to provide context and engage viewers.

- **Graphics and Overlays:** Explore techniques for adding graphics, images, and overlays to enhance your video's visual appeal.

8. **Exporting and Saving:**

- **File Formats:** Learn about different video file formats and how to choose the appropriate format for your video based on your intended use (e.g., YouTube).

- **Export Settings:** Understand the export settings, including resolution, bitrate, and compression, to achieve the best video quality for online streaming.

9. **Uploading to YouTube:**

- **Accessing Your YouTube Account:** Understand how to log in to your YouTube account and access the YouTube Studio.

- **Video Upload:** Learn the step-by-step process of uploading your edited video to YouTube, including title, description, tags, and privacy settings.

10. **Video Optimization:**

- **Thumbnail Selection:** Discover how to choose and upload an attractive custom thumbnail for your video.

- **SEO and Metadata:** Learn how to optimize video titles, descriptions, tags, and closed captions to improve searchability and discoverability.

11. **Scheduling and Privacy:**

- **Publishing Options:** Explore the choice between publishing your video immediately, scheduling it for a specific date and time, or setting it to private or unlisted.

- **Monetization and Ad Settings:** Understand how to set up monetization options, including ad placements and revenue sharing.

12. **Engagement Features:**

- **Adding End Screens and Cards:** Learn how to include end screens and cards in your video to promote other content and engage viewers further.

- **Comment Moderation:** Understand how to manage comments on your video and foster a positive community.

13. **Analytics and Tracking:**

- **Monitoring Video Performance:** Explore the analytics tools available in YouTube Studio to track views, watch time, audience demographics, and other metrics.

- **Ad Performance:** Understand how to access data on ad revenue and performance.

14. **Promotion and Sharing:**

- **Sharing on Social Media:** Learn how to share your video on social media platforms to expand your reach.

- **Community Engagement:** Explore techniques for engaging with your audience through comments and community posts.

Editing and uploading your video is the bridge between your creative process and sharing your content with your audience on YouTube.

Chapter 3: Growing Your Channel

3.1 Understanding YouTube Analytics

Understanding YouTube analytics is vital for the success of your YouTube channel. It allows you to gain insights into your audience's behavior, video performance, and growth opportunities. Here, you'll dive into the details of YouTube analytics and how to use it effectively.

Accessing YouTube Analytics:

• **Navigating YouTube Studio:** Understand how to access YouTube Analytics through YouTube Studio, your channel's dashboard for creators.

• **Real-Time and Historical Data:** Explore the distinction between real-time data, which provides immediate feedback on your video's performance, and historical data, which tracks the video's performance over time.

2. **Overview of Key Metrics:**

• **Views:** Learn how to interpret the number of views your videos receive and what constitutes a view on YouTube.

- **Watch Time:** Understand the importance of watch time, which factors into YouTube's algorithm for recommending content.

- **Subscribers:** Gain insights into subscriber growth, including where your subscribers are coming from.

- **Likes and Dislikes:** Understand how likes and dislikes contribute to your video's engagement and how to gauge audience sentiment.

- **Comments and Shares:** Explore the impact of comments and shares on audience engagement and community building.

3. **Audience Insights:**

- **Demographics:** Learn how to access data about your viewers' age, gender, and geographic location.

- **Traffic Sources:** Understand where your viewers are coming from, whether through YouTube search, external websites, or social media.

- **Device and Browser Information:** Gain insights into the devices and browsers your viewers use to access your content.

4. **Engagement Metrics:**

• **Audience Retention:** Explore the audience retention graph and how it reveals where viewers drop off in your videos.

• **Average View Duration:** Learn how to interpret this metric, which indicates how long viewers typically watch your videos.

• **Click-Through Rate (CTR):** Understand CTR, which measures how often viewers click on your video's thumbnail relative to impressions.

• **End Screen and Card Clicks:** Explore data on how often end screens and cards are clicked by viewers.

5.   **Revenue and Monetization Metrics:**

• **Estimated Revenue:** Learn how to track your estimated ad revenue and the factors that affect it.

• **Ad Types:** Explore the types of ads displayed on your videos, such as skippable ads, non-skippable ads, and more.

• **Transaction Revenue:** Understand how merchandise shelf, Super Chat, and channel memberships contribute to your revenue.

6.   **Discovery and Traffic Sources:**

- **Search Terms:** Learn which search terms are leading viewers to your content and how to optimize for search.

- **Suggested Videos:** Understand how videos are suggested to viewers, and how to increase your video's chances of being recommended.

- **Browse Features:** Explore how videos are discovered through YouTube's homepage and subscriptions feed.

7. **Advanced Metrics and Reports:**

- **Playback Locations:** Discover where your videos are being watched, whether on YouTube's platform, embedded on websites, or on mobile devices.

- **Traffic Sources:** Analyze which external websites and social media platforms are driving traffic to your channel.

- **Revenue Reports:** Delve into detailed revenue reports, including ad revenue, transaction revenue, and AdSense earnings.

8. **Audience Retention Strategies:**

- **Analyzing Drop-Off Points:** Learn how to identify where viewers lose interest in your videos and develop strategies to maintain their engagement.

• **Optimizing Content Length:** Understand how to strike a balance between video length and viewer retention.

• **End Screens and Cards:** Explore how to strategically use end screens and cards to direct viewers to more of your content.

9. Using Analytics to Improve Content:

• **Content Insights:** Learn how to apply analytics to improve your content strategy, including creating content that resonates with your audience.

• **A/B Testing:** Explore how to conduct A/B testing to assess the impact of different video elements on viewer engagement.

• **Strategies for Growth:** Understand how analytics can inform your growth strategy, such as identifying opportunities to expand your audience or create content on trending topics.

Understanding YouTube analytics is a valuable skill that empowers you to make data-driven decisions and enhance your content strategy.

- ## 3.2 Promoting Your Videos

Promoting your videos is essential for growing your YouTube channel's audience and increasing your reach. This part of the book will teach you a variety of methods and approaches for marketing your videos. Here's a comprehensive breakdown of what you can expect to learn:

1. **Optimizing Video Titles, Descriptions, and Tags:**

- **Keyword Research:** Understand the importance of keyword research to identify the search terms and phrases your target audience is using.

- **Optimizing Titles:** Learn how to create compelling and keyword-rich video titles that both attract viewers and are search engine-friendly.

- **Writing Descriptions:** Explore techniques for crafting informative, engaging, and keyword-rich video descriptions.

- **Tagging Videos:** Understand how to select relevant tags that enhance the discoverability of your videos and attract a wider audience.

2. **Thumbnail Design and Optimization:**

- **Thumbnail Creation:** Learn how to design visually compelling and click-worthy thumbnails that encourage viewers to click on your videos.

• **A/B Testing:** Understand the concept of A/B testing for thumbnails to determine which designs are most effective at capturing viewers' attention.

3. **Utilizing End Screens and Cards:**

• **End Screens:** Discover how to use end screens effectively to direct viewers to other videos on your channel, playlists, or subscribe buttons.

• **Cards:** Learn how to add interactive cards within your videos to promote other content or external websites.

4. **Sharing on Social Media:**

• **Social Media Platforms:** Understand the importance of sharing your videos on various social media platforms to expand your reach.

• **Optimizing Posts:** Learn how to create engaging and informative social media posts that entice your followers to click through and watch your video.

5. **Engaging with the YouTube Community:**

• **Comments and Community Posts:** Understand the significance of engaging with your viewers through comments and community posts on your channel.

- **Collaborations:** Explore the benefits of collaborating with other content creators to tap into their audience and introduce your content to new viewers.

6. **Email Marketing and Newsletters:**

- **Building an Email List:** Learn how to build and maintain an email list of subscribers who are interested in your content.

- **Sending Video Updates:** Discover how to use email newsletters to send video updates and engage with your subscribers directly.

7. **Participating in Online Communities:**

- **Forums and Groups:** Understand how to engage with online forums, groups, and communities that align with your niche, and share your videos when appropriate.

- **Subreddits and Niche Platforms:** Learn how to participate in subreddits, niche-specific platforms, and other online communities that welcome content sharing.

8. **Cross-Promotion:**

- **Leveraging Other Platforms:** Explore cross-promotion opportunities, such as promoting your YouTube channel on your blog, website, or other online platforms where you have a presence.

- **Utilizing Business Cards and Merchandise:** Learn about physical forms of cross-promotion, such as including your channel information on business cards or merchandise.

9. **Engaging with Viewers:**

- **Live Streams and Q&A Sessions:** Discover how to engage with your viewers through live streams, Q&A sessions, and real-time interactions.

- **Listener Feedback:** Learn how to use audience feedback and requests to shape your content and foster a sense of community.

10. **Promotional Strategies:**

- **Collaborations:** Explore the power of collaborations with other content creators to tap into their audiences and expand your reach.

- **Content Series:** Understand the concept of content series, where each video builds on the last, encouraging viewers to watch multiple videos.

11. Paid Promotion and Advertising:

• **YouTube Ads:** Learn about promoting your videos through YouTube's advertising platform, including in-stream ads and discovery ads.

• **Other Advertising Platforms:** Explore the potential benefits of promoting your videos on other advertising platforms, such as Facebook or Instagram.

12. Tracking and Analyzing Promotion Efforts:

• **Measuring Impact:** Understand how to track and measure the impact of your promotional efforts, including monitoring traffic sources and engagement rates.

• **Adjusting Strategies:** Learn how to adapt your promotion strategies based on data and insights gathered from your analytics.

3.3 Collaborating with Other YouTubers

Collaborating with other YouTubers is a powerful way to grow your channel, expand your audience, and create engaging content. Let's explore the ins and outs of collaborating with fellow content creators on YouTube.

Identifying Collaborative Opportunities:

• **Complementary Niches:** Understand how to identify content creators in niches that complement or overlap with your own, providing a natural fit for collaboration.

• **Similar Audience:** Consider partnering with YouTubers who share a similar target audience, making it more likely that their viewers will be interested in your content.

2. Approaching Potential Collaborators:

• **Initial Contact:** Learn how to reach out to potential collaborators through social media, email, or other communication channels, and how to craft a compelling message.

• **Building Rapport:** Understand the importance of building a relationship with your potential collaborator before discussing specific collaboration ideas.

3. Types of Collaborations:

• **Co-Hosted Videos:** Explore the concept of creating videos together, whether it's a discussion, challenge, or tutorial.

• **Guest Appearances:** Consider having another content creator as a guest on your channel or appearing as a guest on theirs.

- **Collaborative Projects:** Learn about larger collaborative projects, such as series, podcasts, or charity events.

- **Shoutouts and Cross-Promotion:** Understand how to cross-promote each other's channels through shoutouts, channel links, or video annotations.

4. **Planning the Collaboration:**

- **Setting Goals:** Define the goals and objectives of the collaboration, such as expanding your reach, creating entertaining content, or providing educational value.

- **Content Planning:** Plan the content you'll create together, including the format, structure, and theme of the video or series.

- **Scheduling:** Coordinate the timing of the collaboration, ensuring both parties have ample time to prepare and promote the video.

5. **Collaborative Video Creation:**

- **Recording:** Explore the logistics of recording a collaborative video, whether it's done in person, through video conferencing, or by combining separately recorded segments.

• **Script or Outline:** Develop a shared script or outline that both collaborators can follow to ensure a structured and engaging video.

• **Roles and Responsibilities:** Define the roles and responsibilities of each collaborator, which might include hosting, guest appearances, or specific tasks.

6. **Cross-Promotion and Promotion Strategies:**

• **Promotion Plan:** Develop a promotion plan for the collaboration, including how and when both collaborators will promote the video.

• **Cross-Promotion Assets:** Create promotional assets, such as custom thumbnails, social media posts, and teasers, to help promote the collaboration.

• **Engaging Your Audience:** Encourage your audience to engage with the collaboration, such as by leaving comments, liking, sharing, and subscribing to the collaborating channel.

7. **Resolving Differences and Disputes:**

• **Effective Communication:** Learn how to effectively communicate and resolve any differences or disputes that may arise during the collaboration process.

• **Agreements and Contracts:** Understand the importance of clear agreements and contracts, especially for larger collaborative projects, to protect all parties involved.

8. **Post-Collaboration Activities:**

• **Collaboration Playlists:** Consider creating playlists that feature all the collaborative videos you've done with different creators, making it easier for viewers to discover them.

• **Continued Collaboration:** Explore the possibility of continuing collaborations with content creators you've worked with before, creating an ongoing relationship.

9. **Analyzing the Collaboration's Impact:**

• **Tracking Metrics:** Learn how to track the impact of the collaboration through analytics, such as increased subscribers, views, and audience engagement.

• **Adjusting Future Collaborations:** Use the insights gained from past collaborations to inform your approach to future partnerships.

Collaborating with other YouTubers is an effective way to grow your channel and create engaging content that appeals to a broader audience.

Chapter 4: Building Your Audience

4.1 Engaging with Your Viewers

Engaging with your viewers is a fundamental aspect of building a successful YouTube channel. It fosters a sense of community, strengthens viewer loyalty, and encourages audience growth.

Importance of Viewer Engagement:

• **Community Building:** Understand how engaging with your viewers contributes to building a sense of community around your channel.

• **Audience Loyalty:** Learn how engagement helps foster viewer loyalty and encourages them to return to your channel for more content.

2. **Comment Interaction:**

• **Monitoring Comments:** Learn how to monitor and manage comments on your videos, including how to filter spam and inappropriate comments.

• **Timely Responses:** Discover the value of responding to comments promptly, acknowledging viewer feedback, and fostering a two-way conversation.

3.   Moderation and Comment Policies:

•   **Setting Comment Policies:** Consider establishing clear comment policies on your channel to maintain a positive and respectful comment section.

•   **Moderation Tools:** Explore moderation tools and settings within YouTube to maintain a constructive comment environment.

4.   Community Posts and Updates:

•   **Creating Community Posts:** Understand how to use YouTube's community tab to create posts, polls, and updates to engage with your audience.

•   **Updates and Teasers:** Use community posts to share channel updates, teasers for upcoming content, and insights into your creative process.

5.   Live Streaming and Real-Time Interaction:

•   **Live Chat:** Learn how to engage with viewers in real time during live streams, including reading and responding to chat messages.

•   **Q&A Sessions:** Consider hosting live Q&A sessions to directly address viewer questions and foster a sense of connection.

6. Feedback and Audience Input:

• **Listening to Feedback:** Understand the importance of listening to viewer feedback and using it to improve your content and channel.

• **Viewer Input:** Encourage viewer input on content ideas, video topics, and the direction of your channel.

7. Community Engagement Initiatives:

• **Contests and Giveaways:** Explore the concept of hosting contests and giveaways as a way to engage with your audience and show appreciation.

• **Viewer Challenges:** Consider creating challenges or activities that involve your viewers, encouraging them to participate and share their experiences.

8. Responding to Criticism and Negative Feedback:

• **Constructive Feedback:** Learn how to differentiate between constructive criticism and negative comments, and respond appropriately to each.

• **Maintaining Professionalism:** Understand the importance of maintaining professionalism and not engaging in online conflicts or arguments.

9.   Audience Surveys and Polls:

•   **Gauging Viewer Interests:** Learn how to conduct audience surveys and polls to gauge viewer interests, preferences, and opinions.

•   **Content Decision-Making:** Use the insights gathered from surveys and polls to inform your content decisions and strategy.

10.   Thanking Your Audience:

•   **Appreciation Videos:** Consider creating special videos to express your gratitude and appreciation to your viewers for their support.

•   **Milestones and Celebrations:** Acknowledge channel milestones and celebrate achievements with your audience.

11.   Cross-Promotion and Shoutouts:

•   **Promoting Viewer Content:** Explore the idea of promoting viewer content or channels as a way to show appreciation and engage with your audience.

•   **Collaboration Opportunities:** Consider offering shoutouts to active and engaged viewers as a form of recognition.

12.   Balancing Viewer Engagement:

•   **Time Management:** Learn how to balance your time between content creation and viewer engagement, ensuring you have the capacity to do both effectively.

•   **Setting Boundaries:** Understand the importance of setting boundaries and being realistic about the level of engagement you can maintain.

Engaging with your viewers is a dynamic and rewarding aspect of being a content creator on YouTube.

4.2 Building a community

Building a community around your YouTube channel is a powerful way to foster audience engagement, increase viewer loyalty, and enhance your overall YouTube experience. Let's explore the strategies and techniques for effectively building a community on YouTube:

Understanding Community Building:

•   **Community vs. Audience:** Differentiate between your audience (viewers) and your community (engaged and loyal viewers who actively participate in your channel's activities).

• **The Power of Community:** Recognize the value of building a community that goes beyond passive viewership and includes interaction and connection.

2. **Consistent Branding and Channel Identity:**

• **Branding Elements:** Establish consistent branding elements for your channel, including logos, colors, banners, and visual motifs.

• **Channel Identity:** Define your channel's identity and the core message or theme that your content conveys.

3. **Community Engagement Initiatives:**

• **Community Posts:** Make use of YouTube's community tab to post updates, polls, and content teasers, allowing you to engage directly with your audience.

• **Q&A Sessions:** Host live Q&A sessions to interact with your viewers in real time and answer their questions.

• **Exclusive Content:** Consider offering exclusive content, such as behind-the-scenes footage or bonus videos, to reward your most dedicated community members.

4. **Responding to Comments and Feedback:**

• **Timely Responses:** Respond promptly to comments on your videos, fostering a sense of connection with your viewers.

• **Acknowledging Feedback:** Show appreciation for viewer feedback and suggestions by implementing changes and improvements based on their input.

5. **Moderation and Community Guidelines:**

• **Establish Guidelines:** Define clear community guidelines and comment policies to maintain a positive and respectful environment in your channel's comment section.

• **Moderation Tools:** Use YouTube's moderation tools to manage comments effectively and enforce your community guidelines.

6. **Community-Driven Content:**

• **Collaborative Projects:** Collaborate with your community on content creation, involving them in video ideas, challenges, or audience participation.

• **Viewer Suggestions:** Act on viewer suggestions for video topics, challenges, or special projects to demonstrate that you value their input.

7. **Live Interaction and Events:**

- **Live Streams:** Host live streams to connect with your community in real time, discussing various topics or even collaborating on creative projects.

- **Live Events:** Consider organizing live events or online meetups to bring your community together and celebrate milestones.

8. **Recognition and Appreciation:**

- **Shoutouts:** Recognize and appreciate active and engaged community members with shoutouts or features in your videos.

- **Viewers' Content Promotion:** Promote your viewers' content or channels as a way of showing gratitude for their support and contributions.

9. **Social Media and Community Building:**

- **Social Media Platforms:** Utilize various social media platforms to connect with your community outside of YouTube, sharing updates, engaging in discussions, and creating a more extensive online presence.

- **Community Hashtags:** Create and promote community-specific hashtags on social media to unite your viewers and encourage discussion.

10. Viewer Meetups and Fan Events:

• **In-Person Meetups:** Organize in-person meetups or fan events for your community members who are geographically close, allowing for face-to-face interactions.

• **Virtual Gatherings:** Host virtual meetups or online events for your global community, enabling fans from all over the world to participate.

11. Community Guidelines and Expectations:

• **Communicate Expectations:** Clearly communicate your expectations for community behavior, emphasizing respect, positivity, and constructive feedback.

• **Enforcing Guidelines:** Consistently enforce your community guidelines to maintain a respectful and safe environment.

12. Feedback and Community Input:

• **Feedback Channels:** Create designated channels or forms for viewers to provide feedback, suggestions, and ideas.

• **Audience Input:** Act on the feedback and input received from your community, demonstrating your commitment to their needs and preferences.

Building a community around your YouTube channel not only enhances viewer engagement but also creates a supportive and loyal audience.

4.3 Audience Retention Strategies

Audience retention is a critical metric on YouTube because it directly impacts your video's performance and its ability to attract and retain viewers. Keeping your audience engaged throughout your video can lead to higher watch time, improved search rankings, and increased visibility on the platform. Here are some detailed strategies for improving audience retention on YouTube:

1. **Hook Your Viewers Early**:

• Begin your video with a strong, attention-grabbing hook. Your first 15 seconds are crucial. Use a compelling question, a shocking statement, or a teaser to keep viewers interested from the start.

2. **Create Engaging Content**:

• Ensure your video content is interesting and valuable to your target audience. Know your viewers and cater to their interests and needs.

3. Maintain a Clear Structure:

• Organize your content into a logical structure. Use an introduction, body, and conclusion format. This helps viewers follow along and anticipate what's coming next.

4. Editing and Pacing:

• Keep your videos concise and to the point. Avoid unnecessary rambling or long-winded introductions. Edit out pauses and dead air to maintain a good pacing throughout the video.

5. Use Visual and Auditory Elements:

• Incorporate graphics, animations, B-rolls, and other visual aids to make your video more engaging. Visual variety can help sustain interest.

6. Interactive Elements:

• Encourage viewer interaction through polls, questions, or challenges. This can boost engagement and retain viewers throughout the video.

7. Script Your Content:

• A well-prepared script can help you stay on topic and avoid unnecessary tangents. Rehearse your script to sound natural and engaging.

8. Tell a Story:

- People love stories. If your video allows for it, use storytelling techniques to capture your audience's attention and keep them hooked.

9. **Use Captions and Subtitles**:

- Including captions and subtitles can make your content accessible to a broader audience, and it can also help retain viewers who prefer to read along.

10. **End on a High Note**:

- Finish your video with a strong conclusion. Summarize the main points, provide a clear call to action, or tease the next video in a series to keep viewers engaged.

11. **Thumbnail and Title Optimization**:

- Your video's thumbnail and title are the first things viewers see. Ensure they accurately represent your content and pique curiosity.

12. **Upload Schedule**:

- Keep a regular posting schedule so that your audience will know when to anticipate new posts. Maintaining consistency might entice viewers to return for more.

13. **Engage with Comments**:

• Respond to comments on your videos. This interaction can foster a sense of community and encourage viewers to return for future content.

14. Analyze Audience Retention Metrics:

• Use YouTube Analytics to track audience retention data for each of your videos. Identify where viewers tend to drop off and adjust your content accordingly.

15. Collaborations and Shout-outs:

• Collaborate with other YouTubers or give shout-outs to engage with their audiences and potentially gain new subscribers.

16. A/B Testing:

• Try out several video formats, lengths, and styles to determine what your audience responds to the most. Your content can be improved with the use of A/B testing.

17. Cross-Promotion:

• Promote your videos on other social media platforms, your website, or in your email newsletter to bring in more viewers.

Remember that audience retention can vary depending on your niche, target audience, and content style, so it's important to continually assess what works best for your channel. Regularly implementing and testing these strategies can help you maintain and grow your viewership on YouTube.

Chapter 5: Monetization

5.1 Ad Revenue and Partner Programs

Ad revenue and partner programs are crucial aspects of the YouTube ecosystem, especially for creators looking to monetize their content. Let's discuss how ad revenue works on YouTube and various partner programs available to creators.

Ad Revenue on YouTube:

1.   **Ad Types**: YouTube primarily offers two types of ads for generating revenue:

•   **Display Ads**: These are the traditional banner ads that appear above the video player and to the right of the video suggestion column.

•   **Video Ads**: These include skippable video ads, non-skippable video ads, and overlay ads that play before, during, or after a video.

2.   **Monetization Eligibility**: To start earning ad revenue on YouTube, you need to meet certain eligibility criteria, including:

•   Having at least 1,000 subscribers.

•   Reaching 4,000 watch hours in the previous year.

•   Complying with YouTube's policies and guidelines.

3. **AdSense Account**: Creators need an AdSense account to receive ad revenue. AdSense is Google's advertising platform, and it's linked to your YouTube channel to ensure you get paid.

4. **Ad Revenue Split**: YouTube shares ad revenue with creators through the YouTube Partner Program (YPP). The typical revenue split is 55% for creators and 45% for YouTube. This means creators earn 55% of the advertising revenue generated from their videos.

5. **Monetization Settings**: You can enable monetization for individual videos or your entire channel. Monetization options include allowing ads, paid content, and channel memberships.

Partner Programs on YouTube:

1. **YouTube Partner Program (YPP)**:

• YPP is the primary program for creators looking to monetize their content through ad revenue. To be eligible, you must meet the subscriber and watch time requirements mentioned earlier.

• Once in YPP, you can earn money from ads, channel memberships, merchandise shelf, and Super Chat during live streams.

2. **Channel Memberships**:

• This feature allows creators to offer paid monthly subscriptions to their audience. Subscribers receive various perks like custom badges, emojis, and exclusive content.

3. Merchandise Shelf:

• Creators can showcase their merchandise directly on their channel, making it easier for viewers to discover and purchase their products.

4. Super Chat and Super Stickers:

• Watchers can purchase Super Chats and Super Stickers to showcase their stickers or messages during live feeds. A portion of the money made from these exchanges goes to the creators.

5. YouTube Premium Revenue: YouTube Premium is a subscription service where members can enjoy an ad-free experience. Creators earn a share of the revenue generated from Premium members' watch time on their content.

6. YouTube Shorts Fund:

• YouTube introduced the Shorts Fund to reward creators for producing short-form content on the YouTube Shorts platform. Eligible creators can earn a portion of the fund based on their video's performance.

7. **Sponsorships and Brand Deals**:

•   While not directly part of YouTube's partner programs, creators can also make money through sponsorships and brand deals. Companies may pay creators to promote their products or services in their videos.

8. **Fan Funding and Crowdfunding**:

•   Some creators use external crowdfunding platforms like Patreon to supplement their income. Fans can pledge money to support their favorite creators in exchange for exclusive rewards.

Understanding ad revenue and partner programs on YouTube is essential for creators looking to turn their passion into a source of income. Keep in mind that the YouTube monetization landscape may evolve over time, so staying informed about the latest updates and opportunities is crucial for long-term success as a content creator.

5.2 Sponsored Content

Sponsored content, often referred to as influencer marketing, is a popular way for content creators and influencers on platforms like YouTube to earn money by partnering with brands to promote their products or services. In this detailed explanation, we'll explore what sponsored content is, how it works, and best practices for content creators.

What is Sponsored Content?

Sponsored content is a type of collaboration where a brand pays a content creator to feature their product or service in a video. The content creator integrates the brand's offering into their content in a way that feels authentic and natural to their audience. The primary goal is to leverage the creator's influence and reach to promote the brand to a wider audience.

How Sponsored Content Works:

1. Partnership Agreement:

• Brands typically approach content creators with a proposal for a sponsored video. Creators can also reach out to brands they want to collaborate with. Both parties negotiate terms, compensation, and content expectations.

2. Disclosure and Transparency:

• Content creators are legally required to disclose when their content is sponsored. This can be done by adding clear disclaimers in the video description, verbally mentioning the sponsorship in the video, and using YouTube's built-in sponsorship disclosure tool.

3.   Content Creation:

•   The content creator produces a video that seamlessly integrates the sponsored product or service. It's essential to maintain the creator's unique style and voice to ensure authenticity and maintain the trust of the audience.

4.   Submission and Approval:

•   The content is shared with the brand for approval. Brands typically want to ensure that their product is presented in a positive light and aligns with their marketing goals.

5.   Video Release:

•   Once approved, the sponsored video is uploaded to the creator's channel and made public. It's shared with the creator's audience, and the brand may also promote it through their channels.

6.   Compensation:

•   Creators are compensated for their work, and the payment structure varies. Compensation can be a fixed fee, a commission on sales, free products, or a combination of these.

Best Practices for Sponsored Content:

1.   **Relevance**: Choose sponsorships that align with your channel's niche and the interests of your audience. Promoting products or services that resonate with your viewers will feel more natural.

2.   **Authenticity**: Maintain your authentic voice and style. Your audience follows you for your unique content, so any sponsored content should blend seamlessly with your usual videos.

3.   **Transparency**: Always disclose that your content is sponsored. Transparency is not only required by law but also builds trust with your audience.

4.   **Honesty**: Provide an honest assessment of the product or service. If there are drawbacks or limitations, don't hesitate to mention them, as this adds credibility to your endorsement.

5.   **Quality**: Ensure that the sponsored content is of the same high quality as your regular videos. Brands want their products to be presented well, and your viewers expect a certain level of production quality.

6.   **Engagement**: Encourage interaction with your audience. Ask for their opinions, questions, or experiences related to the sponsored content in the video and comments.

7. **Long-Term Relationships**: Building ongoing relationships with brands can lead to more consistent income and opportunities. Brands often prefer to work with creators who have a history of successful collaborations.

8. **Legal Compliance**: Familiarize yourself with the laws and guidelines governing sponsored content in your region. This includes understanding disclosure requirements and the responsibility to follow advertising standards.

Sponsored content can be a lucrative revenue stream for content creators on YouTube, but it should be approached with care and transparency to maintain the trust and engagement of your audience. Building authentic partnerships and delivering high-quality, relevant content is key to successful sponsored collaborations.

5.3 Merchandise and Affiliate Marketing

Merchandise and affiliate marketing are two additional monetization strategies for content creators on YouTube. These methods allow creators to generate income beyond traditional ad revenue and sponsorships. Here's a detailed explanation of both:

5.3.1 Merchandise:

Merchandise refers to products branded with a creator's name, logo, catchphrase, or other elements related to their content. These items are typically sold to the creator's audience, offering fans a way to connect with their favorite content creators and support them financially. Merchandise can include a wide range of products, from clothing to accessories to digital goods.

How Merchandise Works:

1.   Design and Production:

•   Creators collaborate with designers, artists, or merch companies to create unique designs that resonate with their brand and audience. This can include custom graphics, logos, slogans, or illustrations.

2.   Product Selection:

•   Creators decide on the types of products to offer. Common merchandise items include t-shirts, hoodies, posters, phone cases, mugs, and digital products like eBooks or presets.

3.   E-commerce Platform:

•   Creators typically use e-commerce platforms like Teespring, Printful, or their website to set up an online store. These platforms handle product creation, printing, shipping, and customer service.

4.   **Promotion**:

•   Creators promote their merchandise in their YouTube videos, social media, and other online channels. They may also host giveaways, limited-time offers, or discounts to incentivize purchases.

5.   **Fulfillment and Shipping**:

•   When a viewer makes a purchase, the e-commerce platform takes care of printing, packing, and shipping the product directly to the customer.

6.   **Revenue**:

•   Creators earn a profit from merchandise sales after production and platform fees are deducted. The amount earned can vary depending on the product's price and the number of sales.

5.3.2 Affiliate Marketing:

Affiliate marketing involves promoting products or services from other companies and earning a commission for each sale or action driven through your referral. Creators can partner with brands, share affiliate links, and earn money when their viewers make a purchase or take a specified action.

How Affiliate Marketing Works:

1.   Affiliate Programs:

• Creators join affiliate programs offered by companies or brands in their niche. These programs provide unique tracking links and marketing materials.

2.   Product Selection:

• Creators choose products or services to promote that align with their content and audience's interests. They may review, demonstrate, or discuss these products in their videos.

3.   Promotion:

• In their videos and descriptions, creators include affiliate links to the products they're promoting. They may also use banners, buttons, or other visual cues to encourage clicks.

4.   Disclosures:

• Creators must clearly disclose their affiliate relationships in their content, as required by law and ethical guidelines. This transparency is crucial for maintaining trust with the audience.

5.   Commission Earnings:

• Creators earn a commission for each sale or action that results from their affiliate links. Commissions can vary widely, and some programs also offer bonuses for high-performing affiliates.

6. **Payment**:

• Affiliate earnings are typically paid out by the affiliate program on a regular basis, often through methods like bank transfers or PayPal.

Best Practices:

• **Relevance**: Promote merchandise or affiliate products that are relevant to your content and audience. This ensures a higher conversion rate and maintains trust.

• **Transparency**: Always disclose when you have an affiliate relationship or are promoting your merchandise. Honesty is essential for building and retaining your audience's trust.

• **Quality**: Ensure the quality of your merchandise is high. Client satisfaction increases the likelihood of recurring business and word-of-mouth referrals for your goods.

• **Consistency**: Maintain a consistent brand image across your merchandise and affiliate promotions. This helps reinforce your content and message.

- **Diversification**: Consider offering a variety of merchandise items to appeal to different segments of your audience. Likewise, explore a range of affiliate products or services to find the most successful ones.

Both merchandise and affiliate marketing can be effective ways for content creators on YouTube to diversify their income streams while providing valuable products and services to their audience. Success in these areas often comes down to careful selection, promotion, and maintaining transparency with your viewers.

Chapter 6: Legal and Copyright Considerations

6.1 Copyright Issues

Copyright issues are a significant concern for content creators on platforms like YouTube, where original content is created, shared, and monetized. In this detailed explanation, we will explore what copyright issues are, how they can affect creators, and how to navigate copyright-related challenges on YouTube.

6.1.1 What are Copyright Issues?

Copyright issues relate to the unauthorized use or distribution of copyrighted material, such as text, images, music, videos, and other creative works, without the owner's permission. In the context of YouTube, copyright issues typically revolve around the unauthorized use of copyrighted music, video clips, or other media in a creator's content.

How Copyright Issues Impact YouTube Creators:

1.   **Content Removal**: When a creator uses copyrighted material without permission, the copyright owner can request the removal of the infringing content. YouTube's Content ID system often detects copyrighted material and may automatically block, monetize, or takedown videos that contain it.

2.   **Demonetization**: Copyright issues can lead to demonetization of videos. Ad revenue generated by the video may be redirected to the copyright owner, and the creator may not earn from the video.

3.   **Channel Strikes**: Repeated copyright violations can lead to copyright strikes on the creator's channel. Accumulating multiple strikes can result in the suspension or termination of the YouTube channel.

4.   **Legal Consequences**: In severe cases, copyright owners can take legal action against creators for copyright infringement, leading to fines and other legal consequences.

Navigating Copyright Issues on YouTube:

1.   **Understand Fair Use**: Familiarize yourself with the concept of fair use, which allows the limited use of copyrighted material for purposes like commentary, criticism, news reporting, education, or parody. Keep in mind that fair use can be a complex legal concept, and it's advisable to seek legal counsel if you're uncertain.

2.   **Get Permission**: If you want to use copyrighted material in your videos, consider obtaining permission from the copyright owner. This can involve purchasing a license or negotiating terms directly with the owner.

3.   **Use Licensed Content**: Opt for royalty-free music, stock footage, and creative commons-licensed material. Many resources are available for creators to access legally, allowing them to use content without copyright issues.

4.   **YouTube's Content ID System**: Be aware that YouTube's Content ID system automatically scans videos for copyrighted material. If your video is flagged, you can dispute the claim, but be prepared to provide valid reasons for doing so.

5.   **Attribution and Credits**: If you use copyrighted content under fair use, make sure to provide proper attribution and credits. This can demonstrate your intention to use the material legally and ethically.

6.   **Consider Alternatives**: If you're unsure about copyright issues, consider alternatives, such as creating your own original content or seeking collaborations with musicians, artists, or other creators who can provide permission to use their work.

7.   **Use YouTube's Audio Library**: YouTube offers a vast library of music and sound effects that creators can use without worrying about copyright issues. Accessing this library can help you find suitable music for your videos.

8.   **Educate Yourself**: Continuously educate yourself about copyright laws, fair use, and YouTube's policies. Being knowledgeable might assist you in avoiding typical problems or common pitfalls.

9.   **Be Cautious with Public Domain**: Even content in the public domain can have certain restrictions or conditions. Ensure you fully understand the terms before using public domain material.

10.   **Dispute and Appeal**: If you believe a copyright claim is incorrect, you can dispute it through YouTube's copyright system and appeal the decision if necessary.

Remember that YouTube takes copyright issues seriously, and it's essential to respect copyright laws and the rights of content owners to maintain a positive presence on the platform. Familiarizing yourself with these issues and taking necessary precautions can help you create content without facing copyright-related challenges.

6.2 Fair Use and Creative Commons

Fair use and Creative Commons are legal frameworks that offer content creators a way to use copyrighted material and share their own work while respecting intellectual property rights. Here, we will explore both concepts in detail.

6.2.1 Fair Use:

What is Fair Use?

Fair use is a doctrine in U.S. copyright law that allows for the limited use of copyrighted material without obtaining permission from or paying royalties to the copyright owner. It provides exceptions to copyright infringement when specific conditions are met. Fair use is a flexible principle and doesn't have rigid guidelines; instead, it's determined on a case-by-case basis.

The Four Factors of Fair Use:

1. **Purpose and Character of Use:**

• Courts consider whether the use is transformative, meaning it adds new meaning, context, or value to the original work. Non-profit, educational, or commentary purposes are often favored.

2. **Nature of the Copyrighted Work:**

• The nature of the original work is assessed. Factual, non-fiction, or published works may be more conducive to fair use than highly creative, fictional, or unpublished works.

3.   **Amount and Substantiality**:

•   The amount of the copyrighted material used is crucial. Using small portions, less than 10%, may be more likely to be considered fair use. However, this isn't a strict rule, and other factors matter.

4.   **Effect on the Market**:

•   Courts evaluate whether the use of the copyrighted material negatively impacts the potential market for the original work. If the new work serves as a substitute for the original, it's less likely to be considered fair use.

Examples of Fair Use on YouTube:

•   **Critique and Commentary**: Using copyrighted content to provide commentary or critique, such as reviewing a film, music, or a book.

•   **News Reporting**: Incorporating copyrighted material in news reporting, as long as it's relevant to the news event.

•   **Education**: Using copyrighted content for educational purposes, like in classroom settings or educational YouTube channels.

6.2.2 Creative Commons:

Creative Commons (CC) is a licensing system that allows creators to choose how they want their work to be used by others. CC licenses are a way to grant permissions beyond what copyright law automatically provides. CC licences come in a variety of forms, each with unique terms:

CC BY (Attribution): This is the most permissive CC license. It allows others to distribute, remix, tweak, and build upon your work, even for commercial purposes, as long as they give you credit.

1. **CC BY-SA (Attribution-ShareAlike)**: Similar to CC BY, but any derivative works must be released under the same license.

2. **CC BY-ND (Attribution-NoDerivatives)**: Others can download works and share them with proper attribution, but they can't change them in any way.

3. **CC BY-NC (Attribution-NonCommercial)**: Others can remix, tweak, and build upon your work non-commercially, and they must credit you.

4. **CC BY-NC-SA (Attribution-NonCommercial-ShareAlike)**: Others can remix, tweak, and build upon your work non-

commercially, as long as they credit you and license their new creations under the same terms.

5. **CC BY-NC-ND (Attribution-NonCommercial-NoDerivatives)**: Others can download your works and share them, but they can't change them in any way or use them for commercial purposes.

Using Creative Commons Works on YouTube:

When using Creative Commons-licensed content on YouTube:

• Properly attribute the creator as specified in the license.

• Comply with any additional terms specified in the license (e.g., non-commercial use).

• Be aware that some CC licenses may not allow for use in commercial or monetized contexts, so review the license terms carefully.

Understanding fair use and Creative Commons can help content creators navigate copyright issues and responsibly use copyrighted material or share their work with others. However, it's essential to respect the specific terms and requirements of each license and to seek legal advice if you are unsure about how to apply fair use or use Creative Commons-licensed material.

6.3 Protecting Your Content

Protecting your content is crucial as a content creator, especially in the digital age where intellectual property can be easily shared and sometimes misused. Here is a detailed guide on how to protect your content on platforms like YouTube:

6.3.1 Copyright Protection:

1. **Understand Copyright Law**: Familiarize yourself with copyright laws in your country and internationally. This knowledge will help you understand your rights and the protections available to you.

2. **Register Your Work**: In many countries, registering your creative work with the relevant copyright office can provide additional legal protection and evidence of your ownership.

3. **Use Copyright Notices**: Clearly mark your content with copyright notices, which typically include the copyright symbol (©), the year of publication, and your name. This informs others that your content is protected.

4. **Leverage YouTube's Content ID**: YouTube's Content ID system automatically scans videos for copyrighted content. If someone uses

your content without permission, you can apply content claims and choose to monetize, track, or take down the infringing content.

5.   **Watermark Your Videos**: Consider adding a watermark to your videos. This not only promotes your brand but also deters others from reusing your content without permission.

6.   **Secure Music Rights**: If you use music in your videos, make sure you have the appropriate licenses or permissions to do so. You can license music through platforms like Epidemic Sound or use YouTube's Audio Library for royalty-free tracks.

6.3.2 Online Security:

1.   **Secure Your Accounts**: For all of your online accounts—including social media, YouTube, and email—use strong, one-of-a-kind passwords. Turn on two-factor authentication to bolster security even more.

2.   **Be Cautious with Sharing**: Be careful about what you share online. Avoid sharing sensitive personal information that could be used against you, like your home address or phone number.

3.   **Monitor Comments**: Regularly review and moderate comments on your videos to prevent spam

or abusive content. This helps maintain a positive and safe environment for your audience.

6.3.3 Legal Protection:

1. **Understand Fair Use and Copyright Law**: Be well-versed in copyright law and fair use. Understand the principles of fair use to avoid unnecessary disputes and accusations.

2. **Legal Representation**: If your content is infringed upon or if you face legal issues related to your content, consider consulting an attorney who specializes in intellectual property and digital media law.

3. **Contracts**: When collaborating with others, whether it's a brand or another content creator, create clear contracts outlining the terms and conditions of the collaboration, including licensing rights and compensation.

6.3.4 Brand Protection:

1. **Trademark Your Brand**: If you have a distinct brand, logo, or name, consider trademarking it. This offers legal protection against others using your brand for their gain.

2. **Social Media Profiles**: Secure social media handles that match your brand name. Consistent

branding across platforms helps establish your identity and makes it harder for impersonators.

6.3.5 Content Backup:

1.   **Regularly Back Up Your Content**: Always keep backups of your original video files and important data. In case of accidental deletion or unforeseen issues, having a copy of your content ensures you can re-upload it.

6.3.6 Monitor and Take Action:

1.   **Use Tools for Monitoring**: Utilize online monitoring tools to keep an eye on where your content is being used and if it's being misused.

2.   **Enforce Your Rights**: If someone uses your content without permission, take appropriate action. This could include sending cease and desist letters or pursuing legal action if necessary.

By understanding copyright law, maintaining good online security practices, and being proactive in protecting your content, you can create a safer and more secure environment for your creative work. Always consult with legal professionals when in doubt or if you need assistance with copyright protection and enforcement.

Chapter 7: Advanced Tips and Tricks

7.1 SEO and Video Optimization

SEO (Search Engine Optimization) and video optimization are essential strategies for content creators on YouTube to increase the visibility of their videos, reach a wider audience, and ultimately grow their channel. In this detailed explanation, we'll delve into the key concepts and practices associated with SEO and video optimization for YouTube.

7.1.1 SEO for YouTube:

Understanding SEO:

SEO is the practice of optimizing your content, in this case, videos on YouTube, to improve their rankings in search results and attract more organic (non-paid) traffic. Effective SEO involves understanding the platform's algorithms and the user intent behind their searches.

Keyword Research:

1.   **Keyword Research Tools**: Use tools like Google Keyword Planner, YouTube's own search suggest feature, and third-party tools like SEMrush or Ahrefs to discover relevant keywords related to your video topic.

2. **Long-Tail Keywords**: Target long-tail keywords (phrases with three or more words) that are specific to your niche. These keywords are less competitive and can attract a more engaged audience.

Video Title:

1. **Include Target Keyword**: Place your primary keyword as close to the beginning of your video title as possible, as it can positively impact search rankings.

2. **Compelling Titles**: Make your titles compelling and descriptive, offering a clear idea of the video's content to attract clicks.

Video Description:

1. **Keyword-Rich Description**: Include your target keywords naturally in the video description. This helps both viewers and search engines understand your content.

2. **Long Descriptions**: Write informative, detailed descriptions that provide context and additional information about the video's topic.

Tags:

1. **Relevant Tags**: Use tags that are directly related to your video's content. These should include variations of your main keyword.

2. **Avoid Irrelevant Tags**: Avoid using misleading or irrelevant tags, as this can negatively impact your video's search rankings and credibility.

Thumbnails:

1. **Custom Thumbnails**: Design custom and eye-catching thumbnails that represent the video's content accurately. This can improve click-through rates (CTR).

7.1.2 Video Optimization:

Video Content:

1. **High-quality Content:** Produce valuable, interesting, and high-quality content. Your video will rank higher the longer visitors watch it and the more they engage with it (like, comment, share). Create high-quality, engaging, and valuable content. The longer viewers watch your videos and the more they interact (likes, comments, shares), the better your video's rankings will be.

2. **Video Length**: Longer videos tend to perform better, but they must maintain viewer interest throughout. Aim for a balance between length and engagement.

3. **Content Structure**: Organize your video content with a clear structure. Use an engaging

introduction, a well-structured main segment, and a strong conclusion.

4. **Engagement and Interactivity**: Encourage viewers to like, comment, subscribe, and share your videos. Respond to comments to foster a sense of community.

Upload Schedule:

1. **Consistency**: Maintain a consistent posting schedule to help build anticipation and retain your audience.

Video File Information:

1. **File Name**: Name your video file with a descriptive title including relevant keywords before uploading it.

2. **Closed Captions**: Add closed captions to your videos. This increases accessibility and facilitates search engines' comprehension of your video's content.

Annotations and Cards:

1. **Use Annotations and Cards**: Add interactive elements such as annotations and cards to promote related videos, playlists, and websites. This keeps viewers engaged and, on your channel, longer.

End Screens and Video Links:

1.   **End Screens**: Use end screens to promote your other videos, playlists, or encourage viewers to subscribe to your channel.

Playlists:

1.   **Create Playlists**: Group related videos into playlists. This encourages users to watch more of your content and can improve your video's performance.

Mobile Optimization:

1.   **Mobile-Friendly**: Ensure your video and channel are mobile-friendly, as a significant portion of YouTube views come from mobile devices.

Analyze and Adjust:

1.   **Monitor Performance**: Regularly check YouTube Analytics to assess your video's performance. Recognise trends and modify your optimisation and content strategy appropriately.

SEO and video optimization on YouTube are essential for improving the visibility of your content and attracting a larger audience. By conducting thorough keyword research, optimizing your video elements, and consistently creating high-quality content, you can enhance your channel's performance and growth on the platform.

7.2 Livestreaming and Premieres

Livestreaming and Premieres are two valuable features on YouTube that allow content creators to engage with their audience in real-time or with scheduled video releases. In this detailed explanation, we'll explore these features, their benefits, and how to use them effectively.

7.2.1 Livestreaming:

What is Livestreaming on YouTube?

Livestreaming on YouTube allows creators to broadcast live video content to their audience in real-time. It's an interactive way to connect with your viewers, answer questions, host events, and share content as it happens.

Benefits of Livestreaming:

1. **Real-Time Interaction**: Livestreams enable direct interaction with your audience through live chat. Viewers can ask questions, offer feedback, and feel a deeper connection to the creator.

2. **Community Building**: Livestreams help build a sense of community and loyalty among your subscribers, as they often gather for live events and discussions.

3. **Monetization Opportunities**: Creators can monetize livestreams through Super Chat, channel memberships, and advertising, adding an additional revenue stream.

4. **Content Variety**: Livestreams can provide a change of pace from traditional videos and offer a different kind of content that can attract a broader audience.

Tips for Effective Livestreaming:

1. **Plan and Promote**: Announce your livestream in advance to give your audience time to prepare. Promote it on your channel, social media, and other platforms.

2. **Engage with Viewers**: Interact with your audience in real-time by reading and responding to chat messages. Acknowledge your viewers, answer questions, and encourage participation.

3. **Quality Equipment**: Ensure you have good audio and video quality. Consider investing in a decent microphone, camera, and lighting to enhance the viewer experience.

4. **Content Structure**: Plan an agenda or outline for your livestream to keep it organized. Balance entertainment with value for your audience.

5.   **Consistency**: Establish a regular livestream schedule so your audience knows when to expect new content. Consistency helps build an engaged viewership.

6.   **Moderation**: Assign moderators to manage the live chat, keeping it respectful and free from spam or inappropriate content.

7.2.2 Premieres:

What are Premieres on YouTube?

YouTube Premieres is a feature that allows content creators to schedule video releases with a live chat feature. It's a way to debut videos to your audience with a shared viewing experience and real-time interaction.

Benefits of Premieres:

1.   **Scheduled Releases**: Premieres allow you to schedule video releases, build anticipation, and notify your audience in advance.

2.   **Real-Time Chat**: The live chat during Premieres enables creators to engage with their audience during the video's first broadcast, creating excitement and discussion.

3.   **Monetization**: Similar to livestreams, you can monetize Premieres through Super Chat and channel memberships.

Tips for Effective Premieres:

1.   **Announce and Promote**: Let your audience know about the Premiere in advance. Create a teaser or trailer to generate excitement.

2.   **Live Chat Interaction**: Be present during the Premiere to actively engage with your audience in the live chat. Answer questions, provide insights, and thank viewers for attending.

3.   **Community Engagement**: Encourage your viewers to interact with each other and create a sense of community during the Premiere.

4.   **Regular Schedule**: Consistency in your Premiere schedule helps your audience anticipate and attend your video releases.

5.   **Quality Control**: Ensure your video content is of high quality, as you won't have the opportunity to edit during the Premiere.

6.   **Use Cards and End Screens**: Encourage viewers to explore your channel by adding cards and end screens to the video.

Both livestreaming and Premieres offer unique ways to engage with your audience and build a loyal fan base. By effectively utilizing these features, content creators can create memorable, shared viewing experiences and grow their channels.

7.3 YouTube Algorithm Insights

Understanding the YouTube algorithm is crucial for content creators who want to grow their channels and reach a wider audience. The YouTube algorithm determines which videos are recommended to viewers, impacting a video's visibility and success. In this detailed explanation, we'll explore insights into the YouTube algorithm and how creators can use this knowledge to their advantage.

7.3.1 The YouTube Algorithm:

YouTube uses a sophisticated algorithm to recommend videos to users, which includes the following key elements:

1.   **Watch History**: The algorithm considers a user's watch history, understanding their preferences and the types of content they enjoy.

2.   **User Engagement**: Factors like likes, dislikes, comments, and shares contribute to a video's engagement score. High engagement indicates viewer interest.

3. **Video Information**: Metadata (titles, descriptions, tags), closed captions, and user interactions with videos provide essential information for the algorithm to understand video content.

4. **Viewing Behavior**: The algorithm analyzes how much time viewers spend watching a video. A higher watch time indicates that a video is engaging.

5. **Thumbnails and Titles**: Visually appealing thumbnails and enticing titles can attract more clicks, which the algorithm takes into account.

6. **Device and Location**: The type of device and location of the viewer can influence the recommendations.

7. **Subscription Feed**: Videos from channels users are subscribed to appear in their feed, which encourages ongoing viewership.

8. **Notifications**: Users who have enabled notifications for a channel are more likely to see new video releases.

7.3.2 Insights for Content Creators:

To harness the power of the YouTube algorithm, content creators can follow these strategies:

1. **Create High-Quality Content**: Produce engaging, valuable, and well-edited videos. Content

quality is the most critical factor in retaining viewers and encouraging likes, shares, and comments.

2. **Optimize Metadata**: Use relevant keywords in your video titles, descriptions, and tags. This helps the algorithm understand your content and matches it to user searches.

3. **Thumbnails and Titles**: Craft compelling titles and create eye-catching thumbnails that accurately represent your video's content. Misleading titles or thumbnails can hurt your channel's credibility.

4. **Engage with Your Audience**: Interact with your viewers by responding to comments and building a sense of community. Encourage likes, shares, and subscriptions.

5. **Consistent Upload Schedule**: Maintain a consistent upload schedule, as it helps the algorithm predict when your content is relevant to your subscribers.

6. **Watch Time**: Focus on increasing watch time by creating longer videos that maintain viewer interest. Organize your content with clear introductions and conclusions.

7. **Collaborate and Cross-Promote**: Collaborate with other YouTubers to expand your

audience. Cross-promote your content through other platforms and social media.

8. **A/B Testing**: Experiment with different video elements, such as titles, thumbnails, and content, to see what resonates best with your audience. Use YouTube Analytics to gain insights.

9. **Encourage Viewers to Subscribe and Enable Notifications**: Ask your viewers to subscribe and turn on notifications. This can improve their chances of seeing your new videos.

10. **Use Playlists**: Organize your videos into playlists to encourage viewers to watch more of your content, which can boost watch time.

11. **Optimize for Mobile**: Given that a significant portion of YouTube views come from mobile devices, ensure your content is mobile-friendly.

12. **Diversify Content**: Explore different content formats and topics to appeal to a wider audience.

13. **Monitor Analytics**: Regularly check YouTube Analytics to gain insights into your audience, track video performance, and adapt your strategy accordingly.

Keep in mind that the YouTube algorithm is continually evolving, so staying updated on the latest changes and trends is essential. Adapting your strategy and consistently delivering high-quality, engaging content are key to harnessing the power of the algorithm and growing your YouTube channel.

Chapter 8: Case Studies

8.1 Successful YouTubers' Journeys

The journey to success on YouTube is a path that many aspiring content creators embark on, with the hope of building a dedicated audience, making a living, and achieving fame. While every successful YouTuber's journey is unique, there are common elements and stages that many of them go through. In this detailed explanation, we will explore the typical trajectory of successful YouTubers, highlighting the challenges, strategies, and key factors that contribute to their achievements.

8.1.1 Finding Their Niche and Passion:

Successful YouTubers often start with a strong passion or interest in a specific topic or niche. This passion drives them to create content that they genuinely care about, making their videos authentic and relatable. They are inspired by their hobbies, expertise, or a desire to share their unique experiences with the world.

8.1.2 Learning and Experimenting:

The early days of a YouTuber's journey are marked by learning and experimentation. They might not have professional equipment or video editing skills, but they are eager to learn. They watch YouTube tutorials and practice video production and editing, gradually improving their content quality.

8.1.3 Consistency and Commitment:

One of the key factors in their journey is consistency. Successful YouTubers commit to a regular upload schedule, which helps build an audience over time. They understand that consistency is essential for viewer retention and channel growth.

8.1.4 Audience Engagement:

Engaging with the audience is crucial. Successful YouTubers respond to comments, ask for feedback, and actively participate in discussions. This interaction helps create a sense of community and fosters loyalty among their early subscribers.

8.1.5 Video Optimization:

As they gain experience, successful YouTubers learn how to optimize their videos for search and discovery. They understand the importance of video titles, descriptions, tags, and thumbnails in attracting viewers and retaining their interest.

8.1.6 Monetization and Growth:

Once they've built a substantial audience, successful YouTubers explore ways to monetize their content. They enable ads on their videos, participate in the

YouTube Partner Program, and seek additional revenue streams through merchandise, affiliate marketing, and sponsored content.

8.1.7 Overcoming Challenges:

The journey to success is not without its challenges. Successful YouTubers face obstacles such as:

- **YouTube Algorithm Changes**: They adapt to the ever-evolving YouTube algorithm, which can impact video visibility and growth.

- **Competition**: As the platform becomes more competitive, they need to find ways to stand out and offer unique content.

- **Criticism and Negativity**: Successful YouTubers often deal with criticism, negativity, and online harassment. They develop a thick skin and learn to handle feedback constructively.

- **Burnout**: The pressure of constant content creation can lead to burnout. They strive to maintain a healthy work-life balance.

8.1.8 Collaboration and Networking:

Successful YouTubers often collaborate with other creators. These collaborations can help them tap into new audiences and grow their subscriber base. Networking with other content creators can provide opportunities for knowledge sharing and support.

8.1.9 Diversification and Brand Building:

As they grow, successful YouTubers may diversify their content and explore new niches to broaden their audience. They also work on building their personal brand, creating a recognizable and memorable online presence.

8.1.10 Achievement and Recognition:

Reaching milestones, such as hitting a specific number of subscribers or receiving awards, is a significant measure of success for many YouTubers. It is evidence of their diligence and commitment.

8.1.11 Longevity and Sustainability:

Some successful YouTubers continue their journeys for many years, demonstrating that success on the platform can be sustained over the long term. They continue to evolve, adapt, and provide valuable content to their dedicated audience.

The journey of successful YouTubers is marked by passion, dedication, adaptability, and a deep understanding of the platform and its audience. While each journey is unique, these common elements play a significant role in their achievements. It's a testament to the potential of YouTube as a platform for creativity, expression, and even career success. The stories of successful

YouTubers serve as inspiration for countless aspiring content creators, demonstrating that with hard work and determination, anyone can find success on the platform.

8.1.12 Scaling Up and Investing:

As their channels grow, successful YouTubers often face the need to invest in their content creation. They may upgrade their equipment, hire video editors or graphic designers, and invest in marketing to expand their reach. These investments are made with the belief that improving the quality of their content will lead to even greater success.

8.1.13 Audience Feedback and Adaptation:

Successful YouTubers actively seek and listen to audience feedback. They use constructive criticism to enhance their content and make it more engaging. This iterative process of improvement helps maintain a strong connection with their audience.

8.1.14 Brand Partnerships and Sponsorships:

As their influence and audience size grow, successful YouTubers attract the attention of brands and companies. They often enter into partnerships and sponsorships, creating sponsored content that aligns with their niche. These collaborations can provide significant financial opportunities and broaden their exposure.

8.1.15 Navigating Trends and Algorithm Changes:

Adapting to changes in the YouTube algorithm is a continuous challenge. Successful YouTubers stay informed about updates and trends in video content and platform policies. They adjust their content strategies to ensure that they remain visible in search results and recommendations.

8.1.16 Expanding Beyond YouTube:

Some successful YouTubers explore opportunities beyond the platform. They might create and promote their own products or services, launch podcasts, write books, or engage in public speaking. Their YouTube success can serve as a launchpad for a diverse array of ventures.

8.1.17 Achieving Influence and Impact:

While fame and financial success are common goals, many successful YouTubers also recognize the influence they hold. They use their platforms to make a positive impact, whether it's by raising awareness about important issues, supporting charitable causes, or providing educational content.

8.1.18 Creating a Sustainable Career:

The most successful YouTubers turn their channels into sustainable careers. They diversify their income sources, ensuring that they're not solely reliant on ad revenue. This financial stability allows them to continue producing content and investing in their channels.

8.1.19 Helping Aspiring YouTubers:

Many successful YouTubers share their knowledge and experiences with aspiring content creators. They offer tips, advice, and mentorship, helping others navigate the challenges and complexities of YouTube.

8.1.20 Reflecting on the Journey:

As they look back on their journeys, successful YouTubers often acknowledge the hard work, dedication, and resilience that led to their achievements. They understand that the journey to success is not always linear and that there will be ups and downs along the way.

8.2 Lessons from Real-Life Examples

Real-life examples of successful YouTubers can offer valuable insights and lessons for aspiring content creators. These individuals have carved their own unique paths to success on the platform, and their experiences provide a wealth of knowledge. In this detailed explanation, we'll delve into lessons from real-life examples of successful YouTubers.

8.2.1 Casey Neistat: The Power of Storytelling

Casey Neistat, a filmmaker and vlogger, rose to prominence on YouTube by combining his storytelling skills with cinematic visuals. Some key lessons from his journey:

• **Quality Matters**: Invest in high-quality production. Casey's attention to detail in camera work, editing, and storytelling set him apart.

• **Authenticity**: Be yourself. Casey's authenticity and unique style drew in viewers who appreciated his genuine approach.

• **Consistency**: Commit to a regular upload schedule. Casey's daily vlogging format helped build a dedicated audience.

• **Experimentation**: Don't be afraid to experiment with different video formats. Casey's "Snowboarding with the NYPD" video went viral because of its uniqueness.

8.2.2 PewDiePie (Felix Kjellberg): Building a Loyal Fanbase

PewDiePie is one of the most well-known YouTubers, primarily known for his gaming content. Lessons from his journey include:

• **Connect with Your Audience**: PewDiePie's interactions with his audience, including inside jokes and memes, create a strong sense of community.

• **Diversification**: He diversified his content beyond gaming to vlogs, commentary, and humor. This keeps his channel fresh and appealing to a broad audience.

• **Humble Beginnings**: Remember that even the most successful creators started with small audiences. PewDiePie's journey began in his room, just like many others.

8.2.3 Marques Brownlee (MKBHD): Expertise and Authority

MKBHD, Marques Brownlee's channel, is known for in-depth tech reviews. His journey offers these lessons:

- **Expertise**: Be knowledgeable in your niche. Marques' deep understanding of technology earned him respect and credibility in his field.

- **High Production Values**: Invest in quality equipment and production. His videos are known for their professional and sleek presentation.

- **Consistent Branding**: Maintain a consistent visual style and branding to make your channel easily recognizable.

8.2.4 Jenna Marbles: Authenticity and Evolution

Jenna Marbles' channel originally featured comedy and humor. She teaches the following lessons:

- **Authenticity**: Be unapologetically yourself. Jenna's humor and honesty resonated with viewers.

- **Content Evolution**: It's okay to change your content over time. Jenna transitioned from comedy to more lifestyle and personal content, and her audience supported this shift.

- **Address Feedback**: Listening to her audience's feedback and adapting her content accordingly helped her maintain engagement.

8.2.5 The Slow Mo Guys (Gavin Free and Dan Gruchy): Niche Content

The Slow Mo Guys create content in super slow motion. Their journey illustrates the following:

• **Niche Appeal**: Don't be afraid to explore a niche. The Slow Mo Guys' unique concept captured a dedicated audience.

• **Quality Over Quantity**: Rather than frequent uploads, they prioritize high-quality content, which has garnered millions of subscribers.

8.2.6 Emma Chamberlain: Relatability and Relaxed Content

Emma Chamberlain's channel features lifestyle and vlog content. Her journey offers these insights:

• **Relatability**: Embrace your flaws and insecurities. Emma's relatable persona makes her viewers feel like she's a friend.

• **Natural Style**: You don't need a lot of editing or fancy equipment. Emma's vlogs often feature minimal editing and off-the-cuff moments.

• **Consistency**: Maintain a regular upload schedule. Emma's consistency has contributed to her rapid rise on the platform.

8.2.7 Lessons from Diversity:

These real-life examples also highlight the diversity of content and approaches that can lead to success on YouTube. Whether you're interested in tech reviews, gaming, lifestyle vlogs, humor, or slow-motion experiments, there's a place for you on the platform.

8.2.8 Michelle Phan: The Power of Tutorials and Personal Branding

Michelle Phan was through her makeup lesson videos that she rose to stardom. Her journey teaches us numerous important lessons:

• **Tutorials and Education**: Providing valuable, educational content can attract a dedicated audience. Michelle's makeup tutorials helped viewers learn new skills.

• **Personal Branding**: You can stand out by developing a distinctive personal brand. Building a strong personal brand can set you apart. Michelle's distinct style and her ability to connect with her audience on a personal level contributed to her success.

• **Entrepreneurship**: She went on to build her own makeup brand, showing that YouTube can be a stepping stone to entrepreneurial ventures.

8.2.9 Vsauce (Michael Stevens): Curiosity and Intellectual Content

Vsauce is known for its educational and thought-provoking content. Lessons from Michael Stevens' journey include:

• **Curiosity**: Cultivate your curiosity and share your passion for learning. Michael's insatiable curiosity about the world led to engaging educational content.

• **Research and Depth**: In-depth research and well-structured content are essential for intellectual topics. Michael's thorough approach is a hallmark of his channel.

• **Engagement**: Encourage critical thinking and engagement with your audience. Michael's videos often pose intriguing questions and promote discussion.

8.2.10 Liza Koshy: Comedy and Relatability

Liza Koshy is a comedy YouTuber and actress who offers several important lessons:

• **Comedy and Relatability**: Humor and relatability can be powerful. Liza's comedic sketches and relatable content resonated with a wide audience.

• **Character Development**: She created distinctive characters that became fan favorites. Developing unique personas can make your content more memorable.

• **Versatility**: Liza transitioned from short sketches to longer content, showcasing the importance of being versatile and evolving your content.

8.2.11 Lessons from Challenges:

Many of these successful YouTubers faced their share of challenges, whether it was adapting to algorithm changes, overcoming self-doubt, or navigating the complexities of the entertainment industry. These challenges highlight the resilience required to succeed on YouTube.

8.2.12 Authenticity and Being True to Yourself:

One consistent theme among these examples is the importance of authenticity. Successful YouTubers often find their niche by being true to themselves, sharing their unique perspectives, and embracing their quirks and imperfections. Their genuine approach connects with viewers on a personal level.

8.2.13 The Ongoing Journey:

The journeys of these YouTubers are ongoing, with each of them continuously adapting, evolving, and expanding their reach. Their stories serve as a reminder that success on YouTube is not a destination but a dynamic and ever-evolving journey.

8.3 Finding Your Unique Path

Finding your unique path as a content creator on YouTube is crucial for building a successful channel and engaging a dedicated audience. While there's no one-size-fits-all formula, there are several key principles and strategies that can help guide your journey.

8.3.1 Identifying Your Passion:

1.   **Start with What You Love:** The foundation of your YouTube journey should be your passion. Think about what genuinely excites and interests you. It could be a hobby, a skill, a subject you're knowledgeable about, or a creative outlet. Your excitement will naturally shine through in your content.

2.   **Niche Selection:** Once you've identified your passion, consider how you can narrow it down into a niche. For example, if you love cooking, you might specialize in a specific cuisine, dietary preference, or cooking technique. A well-defined niche can help you stand out in a crowded platform.

8.3.2 Audience Understanding:

1.   **Identify Your Target Audience:** Consider the audience that your content is intended for. Content development will be guided by your understanding of the needs, interests, and preferences of your target audience. **Market Research:** Study what other successful YouTubers in your niche are doing. Analyze their content, their audience engagement, and what sets them apart. This can give you insights into the kind of content your target audience might be looking for.

8.3.3 Authenticity and Uniqueness:

1.   **Be Yourself:** Authenticity is a powerful tool on YouTube. Embrace your uniqueness, quirks, and individuality. Your personality and perspective are what make you different from others in your niche.

2.   **Differentiate from Competitors:** Find what makes your content unique. This could be your storytelling style, your approach to tutorials, your humor, or your personal experiences. Highlight this uniqueness in your content.

8.3.4 Consistency and Quality:

1.   **Create a Posting Schedule**: Reliability is essential. Establish and adhere to a posting schedule that suits your needs. Consistent uploads maintain your audience.

2.   **Prioritize Quality:** While consistency is important, never compromise on quality. Invest time in editing, production, and research to ensure your content is the best it can be.

8.3.5 Engaging with Your Audience:

1.   **Build a Community:** Interact with your viewers through comments, live streams, social media, and community posts. Interacting with your audience encourages loyalty and a sense of community.

2.   **Listen to Feedback:** Pay attention to the feedback and suggestions your audience provides. It can help you understand what your viewers want and make necessary improvements.

8.3.6 Adapting to Trends and Algorithm Changes:

1.   **Stay Informed:** Keep an eye on YouTube trends, algorithm changes, and industry developments. Being aware of these shifts allows you to adapt your content strategy.

2.   **A/B Testing:** Experiment with different video formats, titles, thumbnails, and content types to see what resonates best with your audience. Use YouTube Analytics to gain insights.

8.3.7 Collaborate and Network:

1.   **Collaboration:** Partner with other content creators in your niche or related fields. Collaborations can introduce your channel to new audiences and create engaging content.

2.   **Networking:** Attend YouTube and content creator events, conferences, or online forums. Building a network can offer support, advice, and opportunities.

8.3.8 Monetization Strategies:

1.   **Diversify Income Streams:** While ad revenue is a primary income source, consider other revenue streams such as sponsored content, affiliate marketing, merchandise, online courses, or Patreon support.

2.   **Be Patient:** Building a successful YouTube channel takes time. Be patient and persistent, and don't solely focus on monetary rewards in the early stages.

8.3.9 Evolving Your Content:

1.   **Don't Fear Change:** As you grow, your interests and skills may evolve. Don't be afraid to pivot or explore new content formats that resonate with you and your audience.

2.   **Reinvent When Necessary:** If your channel faces stagnation, be willing to reinvent your content

or branding. Sometimes, a fresh start can breathe new life into your channel.

8.3.10 Measuring Success:

1.   **Set Goals:** Define your own measure of success. It could be reaching a specific subscriber count, generating a certain income, or simply educating and entertaining your audience.

2.   **Monitor Analytics:** Regularly analyze YouTube Analytics to gain insights into your audience, track video performance, and adapt your strategy accordingly.

8.3.11 Branding and Aesthetics:

1.   **Consistent Branding**: Develop a recognizable brand identity for your channel. This includes your channel art, logo, and overall visual style. Consistency in branding helps viewers identify your content quickly.

2.   **Unique Aesthetics**: Consider the aesthetics of your videos. The way you present your content visually, including your video thumbnails and on-screen graphics, can set your channel apart.

8.3.12 Storytelling Skills:

1. **Effective Storytelling**: A compelling narrative can elevate your content. Whether you're creating vlogs, educational videos, or entertainment, storytelling skills can captivate your audience and keep them engaged.

2. **Emotion and Connection**: Storytelling allows you to create an emotional connection with your viewers. Share personal experiences, challenges, and triumphs to forge deeper connections.

8.3.13 Accessibility and Inclusivity:

1. **Subtitle and Captioning**: Making your content accessible to a wider audience by providing subtitles and captioning for your videos.

2. **Diverse and Inclusive Content**: Be conscious of creating content that is inclusive and respectful of diverse audiences. Celebrate diversity and treat your viewers with empathy and respect.

8.3.14 Planning and Strategy:

1. **Content Calendar**: Plan your content ahead of time with a content calendar. This helps you stay organized and ensures you're consistently delivering content to your audience.

2. **SEO and Keyword Research**: Understand search engine optimization (SEO) and perform

keyword research to optimize your videos for discoverability on YouTube.

8.3.15 Emotional Resilience:

1.   **Dealing with Criticism**: Be prepared to face criticism and negative comments. Developing emotional resilience is vital to handle such feedback constructively.

2.   **Mental Health**: Prioritize your mental well-being. Success on YouTube can come with pressure, so self-care and maintaining a healthy work-life balance are crucial.

8.3.16 Ethical Considerations:

1.   **Honesty and Integrity**: Maintain ethical standards in your content. Be transparent about sponsorships, disclose any conflicts of interest, and avoid deceptive practices.

2.   **Content Responsibility**: Recognize the responsibility that comes with a YouTube channel. Ensure your content is informative, safe, and respectful, especially when dealing with sensitive topics.

8.3.17 Legal and Copyright Awareness:

1.   **Respect Copyright**: Understand copyright laws and ensure you have the rights to use any third-party content in your videos.

2.   **Licensing Music and Images**: If you use music or images in your content, ensure you have the appropriate licenses to avoid copyright issues.

8.3.18 Evolving Trends and Technology:

1.   **Stay Current**: Keep up with evolving trends and technology. YouTube is constantly changing, and being aware of these shifts can help you stay ahead.

2.   **Tech Upgrades**: As your channel grows, consider upgrading your equipment and editing software to maintain high production values.

Chapter 9: Troubleshooting and FAQ

9.1 Common Problems and Solutions

YouTube content creators often encounter various challenges and obstacles in their journey. This chapter explores some of the most common problems faced by YouTubers and provides practical solutions to overcome these issues.

9.1.1 Content Creator's Block:

Problem: Content creator's block, also known as writer's block, can strike at any time. You might find it difficult to come up with fresh ideas for videos.

Solution:

1.   **Brainstorm Regularly**: Dedicate time to brainstorm video ideas. Keep a notebook or digital document for jotting down potential topics whenever they come to mind.

2.   **Audience Feedback**: Listen to your viewers. Read comments, emails, and social media messages to understand what your audience wants to see.

3.   **Collaborate**: Collaborating with other creators can lead to new and exciting content ideas.

4.   **Revisit Old Content**: Repurpose or revisit older content with updated information, new insights, or a fresh perspective.

5.   **Explore Trends**: Keep an eye on trends, both on YouTube and in your niche, and create content around popular topics.

6.   **Take Breaks**: Sometimes, stepping away from content creation temporarily can help refresh your creativity.

9.1.2 Audience Engagement Issues:

Problem: You may find it challenging to engage and grow your audience, leading to stagnant or slow subscriber growth.

Solution:

1.   **Interact with Viewers**: Respond to comments and actively engage with your audience through social media and community posts.

2.   **Live Q&A Sessions**: Host live Q&A sessions to connect with your audience in real-time and answer their questions.

3.   **Ask for Feedback**: Encourage viewers to provide feedback and suggestions. Show that you value their opinions.

4.   **Create Polls and Surveys**: Use polls and surveys to involve your audience in content decisions.

5.   **Consistency**: Maintain a regular upload schedule to keep your audience engaged and returning for more.

6.   **Community Building**: Foster a sense of community by encouraging discussions and interactions among your viewers in the comments section.

7.   **Offer Value**: Always strive to provide value to your audience, whether it's information, entertainment, or inspiration.

9.1.3 Monetization Challenges:

Problem: Monetizing your YouTube channel may be challenging, and you might not be earning as much as you'd like.

Solution:

1.   **Diversify Income Streams**: Explore various ways to monetize beyond ad revenue. This may include sponsored content, affiliate marketing, merchandise, online courses, or Patreon.

2.   **Optimize Ads**: Maximize your ad revenue by optimizing video length, ad placements, and targeting options.

3.   **Build a Larger Audience**: Growing your subscriber count and view count can increase ad revenue.

4.   **Negotiate Sponsorships**: When working with sponsors, negotiate fair deals that align with your channel's size and niche.

5.   **Consistency**: Consistent content creation and uploading can help grow your audience, leading to increased monetization opportunities.

9.1.4 Burnout and Stress:

Problem: The pressure to constantly create content can lead to burnout and stress.

Solution:

1.   **Establish Work-Life Balance**: Prioritize your well-being by setting boundaries and designating time for relaxation and self-care.

2.   **Schedule Breaks**: Incorporate regular breaks and vacations into your content creation schedule.

3.   **Delegate Tasks**: Consider outsourcing tasks like video editing, graphics, or administrative work to reduce your workload.

4.   **Content Planning**: Create a content calendar to plan and schedule your videos in advance, which can alleviate last-minute stress.

5. **Recharge Creativity**: Engage in activities that inspire and recharge your creativity, such as hobbies, reading, or travel.

9.1.5 Technical Challenges:

Problem: Technical issues with equipment, software, or the YouTube platform can disrupt your content creation process.

Solution:

1. **Regular Maintenance**: Maintain and update your equipment regularly to prevent technical failures during recording or live streams.

2. **Learn Troubleshooting**: Develop troubleshooting skills to address common technical problems that may arise during content creation.

3. **Backups**: Always have backup equipment or alternatives on hand in case of technical failures.

4. **Stay Informed**: Stay informed about YouTube platform updates and technical changes to adapt quickly.

5. **Community Support**: Seek help and advice from online communities, forums, or YouTube tutorials when encountering technical issues.

By addressing these common problems with practical solutions, content creators can navigate the challenges of YouTube and continue to grow, engage their audience, and build successful channels. It's important to remember that persistence, adaptability, and a genuine passion for content creation are essential elements of a successful YouTube journey.

9.1.6 Copyright Issues:

Problem: YouTube's Content ID system and copyright claims can pose challenges to content creators, leading to demonetization or takedowns.

Solution:

1.   **Understand Fair Use**: Educate yourself about fair use and how it applies to your content. Fair use can protect your rights when using copyrighted material for commentary, criticism, or parody.

2.   **Proper Licensing**: If you need to use copyrighted material, ensure you have the appropriate licenses and permissions. This may involve purchasing music or obtaining written consent from copyright holders.

3.   **Use Royalty-Free Resources**: Utilize royalty-free music, images, and video clips to avoid copyright issues. Many resources are available

online that offer content for free or at a reasonable cost.

4.   **Dispute False Claims**: If you believe a copyright claim is erroneous, consider disputing it. YouTube provides a dispute process for creators to address incorrect claims.

5.   **Educate Your Audience**: Inform your viewers about the complexities of copyright on YouTube and the potential impact on your content.

9.1.7 Algorithm Challenges:

Problem: Content creators often face difficulties in understanding and adapting to YouTube's algorithm, which affects video visibility and recommendations.

Solution:

1.   **Stay Informed**: Keep up with algorithm updates and changes by following YouTube's official channels and industry news.

2.   **Optimize Metadata**: Pay attention to video titles, descriptions, tags, and thumbnails. These elements can influence your video's discoverability and performance in search results.

3.   **Engage Your Audience**: Encourage likes, comments, and shares from your viewers. A high

level of engagement tells the algorithm that your content is valuable.

4.   **Watch Time and Session Watch Time**: Focus on increasing watch time, as YouTube's algorithm favors videos that keep viewers on the platform. Create playlists and promote related content to extend session watch time.

5.   **Test and Analyze**: Experiment with different video formats and strategies, and use YouTube Analytics to evaluate their impact on audience retention and engagement.

9.1.8 Legal and Privacy Concerns:

Problem: Privacy laws and legal issues, such as defamation or liability for information provided, can be a source of concern for content creators.

Solution:

1.   **Educate Yourself**: Understand privacy laws and regulations relevant to your content. For example, be aware of data protection laws like GDPR (General Data Protection Regulation) and COPPA (Children's Online Privacy Protection Act).

2.   **Disclaimer and Transparency**: Clearly disclose any potential conflicts of interest, disclaimers, or privacy policies where necessary.

3. **Fact-Check and Research**: When presenting information, ensure that your content is accurate and supported by reliable sources to avoid legal issues.

4. **Legal Consultation**: If you have concerns about the legality of your content, consider seeking legal advice from an attorney experienced in media and online law.

9.1.9 Coping with Platform Changes:

Problem: YouTube frequently updates its policies, interface, and features, which can disrupt your workflow or content strategy.

Solution:

1. **Adaptability**: Embrace change and be flexible in adjusting your content strategy, thumbnails, titles, and other elements in response to platform updates.

2. **Learn and Test**: Familiarize yourself with new features and tools offered by YouTube. Experiment with them to understand how they can enhance your channel.

3. **Community Feedback**: Engage with your audience and ask for feedback regarding the user experience with new platform changes.

4.   **Utilize YouTube Creator Resources**: Take advantage of the resources provided by YouTube, including Creator Insider, Help Center, and Creator Academy, to stay informed about platform changes.

9.1.10 Cybersecurity and Online Safety:

Problem: Content creators may face cybersecurity threats, harassment, or online safety concerns.

Solution:

1.   **Secure Your Accounts**: Use strong, unique passwords, enable two-factor authentication, and regularly update your login credentials to protect your accounts from hacking.

2.   **Online Safety**: Familiarize yourself with best practices for online safety, such as recognizing phishing attempts, protecting your personal information, and using secure networks.

3.   **Blocking and Reporting**: Familiarize yourself with the tools for blocking and reporting abusive users on YouTube. Taking action against harassers can maintain a safe online environment.

4.   **Limit Personal Information**: Be cautious about sharing personal information online. Minimize the exposure of sensitive data in your videos and social media profiles.

By addressing these common problems with practical solutions, content creators can navigate the challenges of YouTube and continue to grow, engage their audience, and build successful channels. It's important to remember that persistence, adaptability, and a genuine passion for content creation are essential elements of a successful YouTube journey. Overcoming these challenges is part of the process, and with dedication and the right approach, creators can thrive on the platform.

- 9.2 Frequently Asked Questions

Frequently Asked Questions (FAQs) are a crucial component of many websites, product manuals, customer support documents, and informational materials. They serve to provide users with quick answers to common questions, thereby enhancing the user experience and reducing the need for direct customer support inquiries. In this article, we'll explore the concept of FAQs in detail, discussing their purpose, benefits, best practices for creating them, and some examples.

1. Purpose of FAQs

1.1 Providing Quick Information: The primary purpose of FAQs is to offer users quick and easy access to information about a product, service, or topic. Users can find answers to common questions without having to search extensively or contact customer support.

1.2 Reducing Support Inquiries: FAQs can significantly reduce the number of support inquiries. When users can find answers independently, it saves both the company and the users time and resources.

1.3 Enhancing User Experience: Well-crafted FAQs enhance the user experience by increasing the perceived value of a product or service. Users appreciate readily available information.

1.4 Building Trust: FAQs can build trust and credibility by showing that a company is transparent and committed to helping users.

2. Benefits of FAQs

2.1 Time and Cost Efficiency: FAQs save time and resources by minimizing repetitive inquiries, freeing up support staff to address more complex issues.

2.2 Improved User Satisfaction: Users prefer self-service options, and FAQs cater to this preference by offering them a way to find answers at their convenience.

2.3 SEO and Website Traffic: Well-structured FAQs can boost SEO by incorporating keywords related to common user queries, attracting more organic traffic.

2.4 Marketing and Sales Tool: FAQs can be used to educate potential customers and overcome objections, helping to drive sales.

2.5 Analytics and Feedback: FAQs can be an excellent source of insights into user needs and concerns. Frequent updates based on user feedback can improve the overall user experience.

3. Best Practices for Creating FAQs

3.1 Categorization: Organize FAQs into categories and subcategories to make it easier for users to find relevant information. Consider using a collapsible or expandable format to keep the page uncluttered.

3.2 Clarity and Conciseness: Responses must to be precise, succinct, and pertinent to the subject at hand. When possible, stay away from technical terminology and jargon. Employ terminology that is easy to understand for the intended audience.

3.3 Regular Updates: FAQs should be kept up-to-date. Ensure that they reflect the most current information about your product or service.

3.4 Search Functionality: Implement a search bar for users to quickly find answers to specific questions.

3.5 Links and References: Include links to related resources, manuals, or contact information for additional assistance.

3.6 User-Focused Language: Write FAQs from the user's perspective. Use "you" and "your" to make it more personal and relatable.

3.7 Analytics and User Feedback: Use website analytics and gather user feedback to continually improve and expand your FAQs.

4. Examples of FAQ Categories

4.1 Product FAQs: Common questions about a product's features, usage, and troubleshooting.

4.2 Service FAQs: Questions related to services, subscriptions, and membership details.

4.3 Account FAQs: Information on account creation, password resets, and managing personal information.

4.4 Shipping and Returns FAQs: Questions regarding shipping, delivery, and return policies.

4.5 Billing and Payment FAQs: Queries about payment methods, invoices, and subscription renewals.

4.6 Technical Support FAQs: Troubleshooting and technical assistance for software, devices, or online platforms.

5. Concluding Thoughts

Frequently Asked Questions are a valuable tool for organizations to enhance user experience, reduce support costs, and improve their online presence. When done correctly, FAQs can be a win-win for both businesses and users. They provide quick access to information while demonstrating a commitment to customer service, ultimately fostering trust and loyalty. Therefore, it's important to invest time and effort in creating, maintaining, and updating your FAQs to ensure they remain relevant and valuable.

6. Content Creation for FAQs

6.1 Use Real Questions: Start by collecting real questions from customer inquiries, online forums, and support tickets. Real questions are more likely to resonate with your audience.

6.2 Provide Detailed Answers: Ensure that the answers to FAQs are comprehensive and thorough. Address the question in detail and, if applicable, include step-by-step instructions, images, or videos.

6.3 Consider the Customer Journey: Think about the different stages of the customer journey. Create FAQs that cater to users at various stages, from those considering your product or service to long-term users.

6.4 Address Common Pain Points: FAQs can be an opportunity to proactively address common pain points or objections that potential customers might have. Use this space to educate, inform, and persuade.

6.5 Keep It Relevant: Don't overpopulate your FAQs with excessive information. Ensure that every question and answer is directly relevant to your product, service, or topic.

6.6 Legal and Privacy Compliance: If applicable, make sure to include information about legal compliance, privacy policies, and terms and conditions.

7. User Accessibility and Design

7.1 Mobile Optimization: Ensure that your FAQs are mobile-friendly. Many users access websites on their smartphones, so a responsive design is essential.

7.2 Clear Navigation: Make sure that the navigation to FAQs is easy to find. Often, a dedicated "FAQ" or "Help" section in your website's header or footer is the best practice.

7.3 Cross-Linking: Link related FAQs within answers to guide users to more information. This keeps users engaged and, on your site, longer.

7.4 Visuals and Multimedia: Sometimes, a picture or video can convey information more effectively than text. Incorporate visuals when they can clarify answers.

8. Maintenance and Updates

8.1 Regular Review: Periodically review and update your FAQs. As your product or service evolves, so do user questions. Keep your FAQs current to avoid misleading information.

8.2 Feedback Mechanism: Encourage users to provide feedback on the FAQs. Create a simple form for users to report inaccuracies or suggest additional questions.

8.3 Announcements and Changes: If you make significant updates or changes to your product or service, make sure to communicate these in the FAQs. This can prevent confusion.

9. Multilingual Support

If your product or service has an international audience, consider offering FAQs in multiple languages. This demonstrates your commitment to serving a diverse user base and can significantly improve the user experience for non-English-speaking users.

10. Integration with Other Support Channels

While FAQs can reduce support inquiries, they shouldn't be the sole support channel. Integrate them with other support channels, such as live chat, email, or phone support. Include links or contact details for users who need personalized assistance beyond what FAQs can provide.

11. Monitoring and Analytics

Leverage website analytics tools to track the performance of your FAQs. Monitor which questions are the most popular, which keywords users are searching for, and where users drop off in their search for answers. Use this data to continually refine and expand your FAQs.

Frequently Asked Questions are a versatile tool that can enhance user experience, reduce support costs, and improve your online presence. By adhering to best practices and continually refining your FAQs, you can create a valuable resource that not only answers common questions but also contributes to building trust and loyalty with your users. Remember that FAQs are not static; they should evolve with your product or service, reflecting the changing needs and inquiries of your user base.

Chapter 10: Beyond YouTube

10.1 Leveraging Your YouTube Success

Leveraging your YouTube success is a critical aspect of building a sustainable online presence, growing your brand, and generating income. Whether you're a content creator, a business, or an individual looking to maximize the potential of your YouTube channel, understanding how to leverage your success is essential. In this detailed guide, we'll explore the strategies and tactics to make the most of your YouTube accomplishments.

1. Building on Your YouTube Success

1.1 Content Consistency

Consistency is key to maintaining and expanding your YouTube success. Regularly upload high-quality content that aligns with your channel's niche and audience expectations. You should let your subscribers know when fresh content is coming.

1.2 Diversify Content

While staying true to your niche, consider diversifying your content. This can attract a broader audience and keep existing subscribers engaged. For example, you can explore new video formats, topics, or collaborate with other YouTubers.

1.3 Engage with Your Audience

Engage your viewers with social media, live streaming, and comments. Creating a community around your channel can help you succeed more on YouTube and fortify your brand.

1.4 Optimize for SEO

Continuously work on optimizing your video titles, descriptions, and tags for SEO. This will help your content rank better in YouTube search results and attract more viewers.

1.5 Track Analytics

Use YouTube analytics to gain insights into your audience's behavior. Analyze which videos perform well, where your viewers are coming from, and when they are most active. Adjust your content strategy based on this data.

2. Monetizing Your YouTube Success

2.1 Ad Revenue

If you're eligible, you can earn money through YouTube's Partner Program by allowing ads on your videos. The more views, engagement, and watch time your channel has, the higher your potential ad revenue.

2.2 Sponsorships and Brand Deals

You might get brand partnerships and sponsorships as your channel expands. Working with businesses can be a great way to make a lot of money, particularly if your content appeals to their target market.

2.3 Merchandise and Products

Leverage your YouTube success to sell merchandise or your own products. This could include apparel, accessories, digital products, or even online courses if you have expertise to share.

2.4 Patreon and Memberships

Encourage your most dedicated fans to support you through platforms like Patreon or YouTube channel memberships. In exchange for a monthly fee, offer exclusive content, early access, or behind-the-scenes perks.

3. Protecting Your Brand

3.1 Copyright and Fair Use

Be aware of copyright laws. Make sure you have the right to use any third-party content in your videos, or ensure your use falls under fair use.

3.2 Trademark Your Brand

If your YouTube channel name and brand are unique, consider trademarking them to protect your identity and prevent others from using it.

4. Expanding Beyond YouTube

4.1 Social Media Presence

Leverage your YouTube success by maintaining a strong presence on social media platforms. Promote your videos, engage with your audience, and reach a wider audience through platforms like Instagram, Twitter, and Facebook.

4.2 Website or Blog

Consider creating a website or blog that complements your YouTube channel. This can serve as a central hub for your content, host additional content, and provide opportunities for monetization through ads or affiliate marketing.

4.3 Public Speaking and Workshops

If your content establishes you as an expert in your niche, explore opportunities for public speaking engagements, workshops, or consulting services.

5. Collaborations and Networking

Collaborating with other YouTubers and content creators can help you tap into their audience and expand your reach. Building a network within the YouTube community can lead to new opportunities and exposure.

6. Legal and Financial Considerations

As your YouTube success grows, you may need to address legal and financial matters, including tax considerations, contracts for sponsorships, and setting up a business entity if necessary. Consulting with professionals in these areas is advisable.

7. Staying Adaptable and Innovative

The digital landscape is constantly evolving. To leverage your YouTube success effectively, stay adaptable and open to innovation. Experiment with new formats and platforms to stay relevant and appealing to your audience.

8. Advanced YouTube Success Strategies

8.1 Utilize YouTube Shorts

YouTube Shorts is a relatively new feature that allows you to create short-form videos, similar to TikTok. Leveraging this feature can help you tap into a younger, mobile-savvy audience. Creating engaging Shorts can lead to increased exposure and potential growth for your main channel.

8.2 Community Tab and YouTube Stories

If your channel is eligible, use the Community tab and YouTube Stories to interact with your audience. You can post polls, updates, and behind-the-scenes content. These features allow you to maintain a more dynamic relationship with your subscribers.

8.3 Live Streaming

Live streaming on YouTube can be a powerful tool for engagement. Host Q&A sessions, interactive events, or live collaborations with other creators. Live streams also contribute to longer watch times, which can positively impact your channel's algorithmic recommendations.

8.4 YouTube Analytics

YouTube offers extensive analytics tools. Dive deep into this data to understand your audience's demographics, watch time, and audience retention. Use this information to tailor your content and posting schedule for maximum impact.

8.5 A/B Testing

Experiment with different types of content, titles, thumbnails, and publishing schedules. Conduct A/B testing to determine what resonates best with your audience. This data-driven approach can lead to more growth and better user engagement.

8.6 YouTube Ad Campaigns

Consider running YouTube ad campaigns to promote your channel or specific videos. While this involves an advertising cost, it can help reach a broader audience, especially if you have a marketing budget.

9. Scaling Your Operations

As your YouTube success grows, you may find it challenging to handle all aspects of your channel on your own. Consider the following:

9.1 Hiring Assistance

You might need to bring in assistance for video editing, graphic design, or community management. Delegating tasks can free you up to focus on content creation and strategy.

9.2 Automate Repetitive Tasks

Use automation tools for scheduling social media posts, managing comments, or tracking analytics. This can save time and make your workload more manageable.

9.3 Establish a Content Calendar

Create a content calendar to plan and organize your video releases, collaborations, and special events. A structured approach helps maintain consistency.

10. Legal and Brand Protection

With increased success, brand protection becomes crucial. Consider these steps:

10.1 Copyright and Licensing

Make sure you have proper licenses for any music, images, or other content used in your videos. This avoids potential copyright strikes and legal issues.

10.2 Trademark Your Channel Name

Trademark your YouTube channel name to protect your brand identity. This can be valuable in the long term.

10.3 Consult Legal Professionals

If you're dealing with complex contracts or facing legal issues, consult with legal professionals who specialize in digital media and intellectual property.

11. Mind Your Mental Health and Well-being

Success on YouTube may come with a lot of pressure. Never forget to give your mental and physical wellness first priority. It's acceptable to take pauses, ask friends and family for help, and, if necessary, even think about therapy or counselling.

12. Stay Adaptable

The digital landscape evolves rapidly. New platforms and technologies emerge, and audience preferences change. Stay adaptable, be open to innovation, and be ready to pivot your content and strategies as necessary to remain relevant.

In conclusion, leveraging your YouTube success requires a combination of content consistency, diversification, monetization, legal protection, and staying adaptable. By applying these strategies and continually evolving with your audience's needs and the digital landscape, you can maximize the benefits of your YouTube channel, turning it into a rewarding and sustainable venture. Remember that building a successful YouTube channel is a long-term endeavor, and patience, hard work, and adaptability are key to your ongoing success.

- 10.2 Expanding to Other Platforms

Expanding to other platforms is a crucial step in diversifying your online presence and leveraging your success on YouTube. While YouTube is an excellent platform for video content, there are various other platforms that can help you reach different audiences, generate additional income, and strengthen your overall brand. In this comprehensive guide, we'll explore the strategies and considerations for expanding your presence to other platforms.

1. Why Expand to Other Platforms

1.1 Audience Diversity

Each platform has its unique user base. Expanding to other platforms allows you to connect with a more diverse audience, which can help grow your overall brand reach.

1.2 Income Diversification

By monetizing your content on multiple platforms, you reduce your reliance on a single income stream, such as YouTube ad revenue or sponsorships.

1.3 Brand Building

Maintaining a presence on different platforms can help you build a more robust and recognizable brand. Consistent branding and content across platforms create a cohesive online identity.

1.4 Traffic Redundancy

It can be dangerous to rely only on YouTube for traffic. Your channel may be impacted by unanticipated events or algorithm adjustments. Adding more platforms guarantees traffic redundancy.

2. Choosing the Right Platforms

2.1 Audience Research

Start by researching the demographics and preferences of users on various platforms. Consider your current audience and which platforms align with your niche.

2.2 Platform Compatibility

Different content is better suited to different platforms. For instance, Instagram is great for visual content, while Twitter is more text-oriented. Adapt your content to the advantages of each platform.

2.3 Competition Analysis

Examine what your competitors or influencers in your niche are doing on different platforms. This can offer insights into where your target audience is most active.

3. Expanding to Specific Platforms

3.1 Instagram

• Share visually appealing photos and short videos.

• Utilize Instagram Stories for real-time updates and engagement.

• Use IGTV for longer video content.

- Collaborate with influencers or brands for sponsored posts.

3.2 Twitter

- Share concise and engaging text-based posts.

- Engage in trending conversations and use relevant hashtags.

- Promote your YouTube videos and blog posts with compelling tweets.

3.3 TikTok

- Create short, attention-grabbing videos that resonate with a younger audience.

- Leverage trends and challenges to boost visibility.

- Cross-promote your YouTube content on TikTok.

3.4 Facebook

- Share video content, articles, and event promotions.

- Participate in Facebook groups related to your area of expertise.

- Consider running Facebook ads to reach a wider audience.

3.5 LinkedIn

• Publish professional articles or thought leadership content.

• Connect with others in your industry.

• Use LinkedIn Live to host webinars and discussions.

3.6 Blogging Platforms (Medium, WordPress, etc.)

• Write in-depth articles related to your niche.

• Link to your YouTube videos and promote your content.

• Engage with the blogging community and gain exposure.

3.7 Podcasting Platforms (Spotify, Apple Podcasts, etc.)

• Convert your YouTube content into audio format.

• Create exclusive podcast episodes or interviews.

• Monetize through sponsorships or listener support.

4. Cross-Promotion and Consistency

Cross-promotion is essential when expanding to other platforms. Promote your presence on these platforms within your YouTube videos and channel description. Similarly, promote your YouTube channel on other platforms to drive cross-traffic.

Ensure brand consistency across platforms, including profile pictures, banners, and content themes. A consistent brand identity helps with recognition and trust.

5. Content Repurposing and Tailoring

While consistency is crucial, don't post the same content across all platforms. Repurpose content to suit the platform's format and audience. Tailor your message to resonate with the platform's users.

6. Regular Engagement

On every platform, interact with your audience by leaving comments, taking part in conversations, and asking for feedback. Participatory involvement cultivates a feeling of belonging and connection.

7. Measuring and Analyzing

Use platform-specific analytics to assess the performance of your content on each platform. Track metrics like engagement, follower growth, and traffic referrals to understand what's working and what needs improvement.

8. Legal and Brand Protection

As you expand to other platforms, remember to protect your brand identity, trademarks, and intellectual property. Trademark your brand name to prevent others from using it without your permission.

9. Stay Adaptable

The digital landscape is continually changing. Stay adaptable and open to new platforms and technologies that emerge. What works today might not work tomorrow, so be ready to pivot your strategies when necessary.

10. Collaboration and Networking

Leverage collaborations with creators or influencers who are active on the platforms you're expanding to. Collaborative content can introduce your channel to a new audience and strengthen your presence on those platforms. Building relationships with like-minded creators can lead to valuable partnerships and opportunities.

11. Paid Promotion and Advertising

Consider allocating a portion of your budget for paid promotions and advertising on other platforms.

Many social media platforms offer advertising options that allow you to target specific demographics and reach a wider audience. These promotions can be particularly effective in gaining initial visibility on a new platform.

12. Content Synchronization

Synchronize your content release schedule across multiple platforms, when possible. This creates a consistent content calendar for your audience and makes it easier for them to follow your updates. Tools like social media management platforms can help automate content sharing.

13. Niche Communities

Explore niche-specific platforms and forums related to your content. Engage with these communities to establish yourself as an authority in your niche and direct interested users to your content.

14. Track and Adapt to Platform Changes

Digital platforms evolve, and their algorithms, features, and user behaviors change over time. Keep yourself updated on these developments and modify your tactics as necessary. Something that was successful on a platform a year ago might not be as successful now.

15. Metrics and Goals

Set specific goals for each platform you expand to. Whether it's follower growth, engagement rate, or referral traffic to your YouTube channel, define what success looks like for each platform. Regularly assess your progress toward these goals and adjust your strategies as needed.

16. Consistent Branding and Messaging

Ensure that your branding and messaging are the same across all platforms. Whether they see your brand on YouTube, Instagram, Twitter, or any other channel, your audience should be able to identify it. This consistency strengthens the identity of your brand and fosters trust.

17. Multilingual Content

If your content has international appeal, consider creating content in multiple languages to reach a global audience. This can significantly expand your viewership and engagement.

18. Quality Over Quantity

While expanding to multiple platforms is essential, prioritize the quality of your content. It's better to excel on a few platforms with high-quality content than to spread yourself too thin and provide subpar content across many platforms.

19. Seek Feedback and Adapt

Regularly seek feedback from your audience on each platform. What type of content do they prefer? How can you improve? Adapt your content and strategies based on this feedback to cater to your audience's preferences.

20. Evaluate and Consolidate

Periodically assess the performance of your presence on various platforms. If you find that certain platforms aren't yielding the desired results, consider whether it's worth maintaining a presence there. It might be more effective to concentrate your efforts on the platforms that provide the most value.

In the dynamic world of online content creation, expanding to other platforms is a strategic approach to maximize your reach, audience diversity, and income potential. Each platform offers unique opportunities and challenges, and adapting your strategies to suit these platforms is key to your success. Remember that successful expansion takes time, effort, and continuous adaptation, but the rewards in terms of audience growth, income diversification, and brand recognition can be substantial.

10.3 What's Next for You?

It is a critical question that individuals, businesses, and content creators should constantly consider as they navigate their digital journeys. This question prompts us to reflect on our goals, ambitions, and strategies for the future. In this comprehensive guide, we'll explore various aspects of planning for what's next, whether you're a content creator or a business looking to capitalize on your digital success.

- **1. Setting Future Goals**

- 1.1 Short-Term vs. Long-Term Goals

- Distinguish between short-term and long-term goals. Short-term goals are immediate targets, while long-term goals are more visionary and strategic. A combination of both is necessary for a well-rounded plan.

- 1.2 Specific, Measurable, Achievable, Relevant, Time-Bound (SMART) Goals

- Use the SMART framework to set goals. This ensures that your goals are Specific, Measurable, Achievable, Relevant, and Time-bound, making them more actionable and easier to track.

2. Evaluating Your Current Position

2.1 Self-Reflection

- Take stock of your current status. What have you achieved, and what could be improved? Assess your strengths and weaknesses, as well as opportunities and threats in your niche.

2.2 Audience and Market Analysis

- Examine your audience demographics and behavior. What content resonates with them? Additionally, analyze market trends and competitive landscape.

3. Diversifying Revenue Streams

3.1 Multiple Income Sources

- Reduce your reliance on a single income source. For content creators, this can mean exploring sponsorships, merchandise, paid memberships, or other monetization avenues.

3.2 Expanding Product or Service Offerings

- For businesses, consider expanding your product or service offerings. This can include new products, subscription models, or digital services that cater to your target audience.

4. Leveraging Emerging Trends and Technologies

4.1 Stay Informed

- Stay up-to-date with emerging trends, technologies, and changes in your industry. This knowledge can help you remain relevant and innovative.

4.2 Experiment and Adapt

- Experiment with new formats and technologies to engage your audience. This might involve adopting VR/AR, live streaming, or interactive content to create a more immersive experience.

5. Collaboration and Networking

5.1 Collaborate with Others

- Collaboration with other content creators or businesses in your niche can broaden your reach and introduce you to new audiences. Partnering with like-minded individuals can lead to new opportunities and innovative projects.

5.2 Attend Conferences and Industry Events

- Participate in relevant conferences and industry events to network with peers and gain insights into the latest developments in your field.

6. Content Strategy

6.1 Content Evolution

• As your audience changes, so should your content approach. Get feedback from your audience on a regular basis, consider their preferences, and produce material that speaks to their needs and interests.

6.2 Content Consistency

• Maintain a consistent posting schedule to keep your audience engaged and informed about your content updates.

7. Legal and Financial Planning

7.1 Protect Your Assets

• Consider the legal aspects of your digital presence. Ensure that your brand identity, intellectual property, and digital assets are protected.

7.2 Financial Planning

• Work with financial advisors to manage and invest your income wisely. Diversify your investments and establish financial security for the future.

8. Expanding Beyond Digital

8.1 Diversify Your Presence

• Consider opportunities to expand your brand beyond the digital realm. This might involve live events, merchandise, or physical locations for businesses.

8.2 Physical and Mental Well-being

• Prioritize your physical and mental well-being. Success in the digital realm should not come at the expense of your health. Develop a balanced work-life routine.

9. Adapting to Changes

• Recognize that change is inevitable. Be prepared to adapt your strategies, pivot when necessary, and embrace innovation to remain relevant in the ever-evolving digital landscape.

10. Continuous Learning and Personal Development

• Make an investment in your career and personal development. Remain enquiring and receptive to picking up new abilities and knowledge.

11. Measurement and Assessment

• Regularly assess your progress toward your goals. Use data and analytics to evaluate what's working and what's not. Adjust your strategies accordingly.

12. Seek Professional Advice

• When planning what's next for you, especially regarding legal, financial, or strategic matters, seek advice from professionals with expertise in your field. A legal consultant, financial planner, or business strategist can provide valuable insights.

13. Staying Resilient

• The digital landscape is dynamic and can be both rewarding and challenging. Stay resilient in the face of setbacks, and understand that success often involves perseverance and adaptability.

14. Innovation and Experimentation

• As you plan your future digital endeavors, make room for innovation and experimentation. Try new formats, platforms, and methods without fear. Innovation frequently results in discoveries and creates new avenues for expansion. Promote originality and creative problem-solving among associates or members of your team.

15. Data-Driven Decision-Making

• Data is a valuable resource in the digital space. Use data analytics to gain insights into audience behavior, content performance, and market trends. Data-driven decision-making can guide your strategies and help you make informed choices about what's next.

16. Personal Brand Development

• For individual content creators, personal brand development is vital. Your personal brand is an extension of your content and should reflect your values, expertise, and unique identity. Invest in building a strong and authentic personal brand that resonates with your target audience.

17. Crisis Preparedness

• In the digital realm, crises can occur, whether it's a controversy, a hacking incident, or a public relations issue. Develop crisis management plans to address unforeseen challenges, protect your reputation, and maintain your audience's trust.

18. Sustainability and Social Responsibility

• Consider how your digital presence can contribute to sustainability and social responsibility. Many audiences value brands and content creators that are environmentally conscious and socially responsible. Align your values with your content and business practices.

19. Global Expansion

• For businesses and creators with international appeal, explore opportunities for global expansion. This may involve translating content, creating region-specific campaigns, or establishing a presence in new markets.

20. Mentorship and Education

• Consider giving back to the digital community through mentorship and education. Share your knowledge and expertise with aspiring content creators or businesses. This not only contributes to the growth of others but can also enhance your reputation and network.

21. Legacy Planning

• Think about the long-term legacy of your digital presence. How do you want to be remembered, and what impact do you want to leave? Whether it's philanthropy, knowledge sharing, or creating a lasting brand, legacy planning can be a motivating factor for your future endeavors.

22. Health and Well-being

- In the fast-paced digital world, maintaining physical and mental health is crucial. Incorporate routines for exercise, stress management, and work-life balance to ensure sustained productivity and well-being.

23. Financial Diversification

- Expand your financial diversification beyond your digital income. Diversify your investments, explore real estate, or consider other forms of income that reduce dependency on a single source.

24. Documentation and Organization

- Maintain thorough documentation and organization of your digital assets. This includes financial records, content schedules, audience data, and contractual agreements. An organized approach ensures efficient operations and risk management.

25. Long-Term Sustainability

- Think about your digital presence's long-term sustainability. How can you ensure that your brand or content remains relevant and appealing to future generations? Stay adaptable and open to evolving with changing audience preferences and technological advancements.

26. Positive Impact and Giving Back

• Consider how your digital success can have a positive impact on the world. Many successful digital entities engage in philanthropic efforts or support causes that align with their values. Giving back not only benefits society but can also enhance your reputation and legacy.

"What's Next for You?" in the digital realm is a multifaceted endeavor that involves a combination of strategic, personal, and ethical considerations. Whether you're a content creator or a business, staying innovative, data-driven, and adaptable are critical factors in achieving sustained success. Beyond personal and financial growth, consider the impact you can have on your audience, community, and the broader world as you navigate your digital journey.

Conclusion

- Recap and Next Steps

Let's recap the key points covered in the discussion so far and outline the next steps you can take to apply these insights effectively.

Recap of Key Points

1. FAQs Best Practices

- FAQs serve as a valuable resource for users, addressing common questions, reducing support inquiries, and enhancing the user experience.

- Start by identifying real questions and crafting detailed, relevant answers.

- Consider the customer journey and address common pain points in your FAQs.

- Keep the content up-to-date, review it regularly, and provide a feedback mechanism for users.

- Ensure legal and privacy compliance when necessary.

- Optimize for mobile devices, maintain clear navigation, and incorporate visuals and multimedia when relevant.

- Monitor and analyze user engagement to continually refine and expand your FAQs.

2. Leveraging YouTube Success

• Consistency and diversification are key to maintaining and expanding YouTube success.

• Explore various monetization avenues, including ad revenue, sponsorships, merchandise, and memberships.

• Protect your brand identity and intellectual property.

• Expand to other platforms to reach diverse audiences and diversify income streams.

• Stay informed about emerging trends and technologies, and adapt your content and strategies accordingly.

• Collaborate with other creators, network, and attend relevant events to foster growth.

• Strike a balance between your long- and short-term goals.

• Seek professional advice for legal, financial, or strategic matters.

3. Planning "What's Next for You?"

• Set specific, measurable, achievable, relevant, and time-bound (SMART) goals for the short term and long term.

- Reflect on your current position, assess strengths and weaknesses, and analyze your audience and market.

- Diversify revenue streams and expand your product or service offerings.

- Embrace innovation and experimentation while staying data-driven.

- Prioritize collaboration and networking to expand your reach.

- Stay adaptable and be prepared to adapt to changes in the digital landscape.

- Invest in personal brand development, legal protection, and financial planning.

- Prioritize sustainability, social responsibility, and well-being.

- Consider global expansion, mentorship, and legacy planning.

- Maintain documentation and organization to manage digital assets effectively.

- Plan for long-term sustainability and a positive impact on the world.

Next Steps

1.   **Identify Priorities**: Prioritize the areas that are most relevant to your current situation, whether you're a content creator, business, or individual seeking to grow your digital presence.

2.   **Goal Setting**: Based on the insights provided, set specific and measurable goals for your digital journey. Consider both short-term and long-term objectives.

3.   **Action Plan**: Develop a detailed action plan for each of your goals. Determine the steps required to achieve them, allocate resources, and establish timelines.

4.   **Monitoring and Evaluation**: Continuously track your progress by utilizing data and analytics. Regularly evaluate your strategies and adjust them as needed.

5.   **Collaboration and Networking**: Actively seek collaborations and build your network within your niche or industry to gain exposure and create opportunities.

6.   **Legal and Financial Considerations**: If necessary, consult with professionals in the legal and financial fields to ensure that you have a solid foundation for your digital endeavors.

7.   **Innovation and Adaptation**: Embrace innovation and be open to experimentation. Experiment with new content formats, platforms, and technologies to engage your audience effectively.

8.   **Personal Growth and Well-being**: Prioritize your personal growth and well-being as you navigate your digital journey. Remember that your physical and mental health are critical to long-term success.

9.   **Brand Development**: If you are a content creator, invest in personal brand development to create a strong, authentic, and recognizable online identity.

10.   **Social Responsibility**: Consider how you can contribute to social responsibility and sustainability through your digital presence. Align your values with your content and business practices.

11.   **Legacy Planning**: Think about the long-term legacy you want to leave with your digital presence. Plan for how you want to be remembered and the impact you wish to make.

12.   **Staying Informed**: Stay informed about industry trends, technology advancements, and

emerging platforms. Adapt to changes and continue learning to remain relevant.

Remember that success in the digital world is an ongoing journey that requires dedication, adaptability, and continuous learning. By applying these insights and taking action on your next steps, you can navigate your digital journey effectively and achieve your goals.

Appendix A: Resources

- A.1 Recommended Tools and Software

Let's explore a comprehensive list of recommended tools and software that can assist you in various aspects of your digital journey, whether you're a content creator, business owner, or an individual seeking to optimize your online presence. These tools cover areas such as content creation, analytics, organization, security, and more.

1. Content Creation and Production

1.1 Video Creation and Editing

- **Adobe Premiere Pro**: A professional video editing software for creating high-quality video content.

- **Final Cut Pro X**: A video editing tool for Mac users known for its advanced features.

- **DaVinci Resolve**: A versatile video editing and color correction software.

- **Filmora**: A user-friendly video editor for beginners and intermediate users.

- **Camtasia**: A screen recording and video editing tool suitable for tutorials and educational content.

1.2 Graphic Design and Image Editing

• **Adobe Photoshop**: The industry-standard for graphic design and image editing.

• **Canva**: A user-friendly graphic design platform with templates for various purposes.

• **GIMP (GNU Image Manipulation Program):** An open-source alternative to Photoshop.

• • **Adobe Illustrator:** Ideal for vector graphics and illustrations.GIMP

• **Affinity Designer**: A vector graphic design software offering powerful features.

1.3 Audio Editing and Podcasting

• **Adobe Audition**: For professional audio editing and podcast production.

• **Audacity**: An open-source, free audio editor.

• **GarageBand**: Mac users can use this for music and podcast production.

• **Reaper**: A cost-effective and highly customizable audio editing tool.

• **Hindenburg Journalist**: Designed for podcasters with intuitive features.

1.4 Animation and Motion Graphics

- **Adobe After Effects**: Ideal for creating motion graphics, visual effects, and animations.

- **Blender**: An open-source 3D content creation suite that includes animation features.

- **Toon Boom Harmony**: Specialized software for 2D animation.

- **CrazyTalk Animator**: Perfect for creating 2D character animations.

- **Pencil2D**: An open-source, easy-to-use animation tool.

2. Social Media and Content Distribution

2.1 Social Media Management

- **Hootsuite**: A comprehensive social media management platform for scheduling and monitoring.

  - **Buffer**: An easy-to-use tool for planning and monitoring social media content.

  - **Sprout Social** is a social media management and analytics tool.

- **Sprout Social**: A social media management and analytics platform.

• **Later**: focuses on Instagram scheduling and visual content preparation.

• **SocialBee**: A tool for content categorization and posting.

2.2 Email Marketing

• **Mailchimp**: A widely-used email marketing platform with automation and analytics.

• **ConvertKit:** Designed for small businesses, bloggers, and creatives.

• **Constant Contact**: Offers email marketing, automation, and e-commerce solutions.

• **GetResponse**: Includes email marketing, automation, and webinar capabilities.

• **AWeber**: A tool known for its email marketing and autoresponder features.

2.3 Content Distribution and Scheduling

• **ContentCal**: Helps plan, schedule, and manage content across platforms.

• **CoSchedule**: Offers content marketing and social media scheduling.

• **MeetEdgar**: Automates content sharing and recycles evergreen posts.

- **IFTTT (If This Then That)**: Creates automated actions between different apps and services.

- **Zapier**: Connects your favorite apps to automate workflows.

3. Analytics and Insights

3.1 Website and SEO Analytics

- **Google Analytics**: The go-to tool for website analytics and user behavior tracking.

- **Google Search Console**: Tracks the functionality of websites in Google search results.

- **SEMrush**: Offers SEO, content, and competitive analysis tools.

- **Moz**: Provides SEO and link analysis for website optimization.

- **Ahrefs**: A comprehensive SEO tool for keyword research and backlink analysis.

3.2 Social Media Analytics

- **Socialbakers**: Analyzes social media performance and provides insights.

- **Brandwatch**: Monitors social media trends and tracks brand mentions.

- **Sprinklr**: Offers social media management and analytics for enterprises.

- **Keyhole**: Focuses on hashtag tracking and social listening.

- **Falcon.io**: Combines social media management with analytics and audience engagement.

4. Organization and Productivity

4.1 Project and Task Management

- **Asana** is a project and task management application designed for teams.

- **Trello**: is a visual project management platform that utilises cards and boards.

- **Basecamp**: A simple and organized project management platform.

- **Monday.com**: A work operating system for teams with customizable features.

- **Notion**: A versatile tool for notes, databases, tasks, and more.

4.2 Time Management and Productivity

- **RescueTime**: Tracks time spent on digital devices and apps.

- **Toggl**: An easy-to-use time tracker for personal and team use.

- **Focus@Will**: Provides music scientifically optimized for focus and productivity.

- **Forest**: A mobile app that encourages focused work through gamification.

- **Todoist**: A task manager with features for productivity and goal setting.

4.3 Cloud Storage and File Management

- **Google Drive:** Provides file sharing, online storage, and teamwork.

- **Dropbox**: A popular cloud storage and file synchronization solution.

- **OneDrive**: Microsoft's cloud storage integrated with Office 365.

- **Box**: A secure file sharing and cloud content management platform.

- **pCloud**: A user-friendly cloud storage and backup service.

5. Security and Privacy

5.1 Password Management

- **LastPass**: A password manager that stores and secures passwords.

- **Dashlane**: A password manager with password generation and digital wallet features.

- **1Password**: Offers secure password storage and management.

- **Bitwarden**: An open-source, self-hosted password manager.

- **KeePass**: An open-source password manager known for its security.

5.2 Antivirus and Malware Protection

- **Norton 360**: A comprehensive antivirus and malware protection suite.

  - **McAfee:** Provides internet security and antivirus programmes.

  - **Kaspersky:** Offers internet security and antivirus programmes.

- **Bitdefender**: Known for its high-quality antivirus protection.

- **Malwarebytes**: Specializes in anti-malware solutions.

5.3 VPN (Virtual Private Network)

- **ExpressVPN**: A trusted VPN service for secure and private internet browsing.

- **NordVPN**: A user-friendly VPN with a strong focus on security and privacy.

- **CyberGhost**: Offers VPN services with dedicated streaming servers.

- **Private Internet Access (PIA):** Recognised for its features that prioritise privacy.

- **Surfshark**: A cost-effective VPN with a strong focus on security.

6. Financial Management and Accounting

6.1 Accounting Software

- **QuickBooks**: A popular accounting software for businesses and self-employed individuals.

- **FreshBooks**: Known for its invoicing, expense tracking, and accounting features.

- **Xero**: Provides accounting and financial management for small businesses.

- **Wave**: A free accounting and invoicing software designed for small businesses.

- **Zoho Books**: A cloud-based accounting solution with features for businesses of all sizes.

6.2 Invoicing and Payment Processing

- **PayPal:** is a popular online payment and invoicing platform.

- **Stripe:** Provides online retailers with payment processing options.

- **Square**: Known for its point-of-sale systems and online payment processing.

- **Wave Invoicing**: Part of the Wave suite, a free invoicing solution.

- **FreshBooks Payments**: Integrated payment processing for FreshBooks users.

6.3 Expense Management

- **Expensify**: Streamlines expense reporting and receipt management.

- **Concur**: Offers expense and travel management for businesses.

- **Receipts by Wave**: Part of the Wave accounting suite, for receipt tracking.

- **Zoho Expense**: Part of the Zoho suite, for expense reporting and approval.

- **QuickBooks Online**: Integrated expense tracking with QuickBooks accounting.

These recommended tools and software cover a wide range of aspects for your digital journey, from content creation and distribution to analytics, organization, security, and financial management. Remember to assess your specific needs and goals to determine which tools are most suitable for your unique requirements. Additionally, explore trial versions or free options when available to find the best fit for your digital endeavors.

Appendix : Glossary

Certainly, an appendix containing a glossary is a valuable resource for providing definitions and explanations of key terms and concepts related to the subject matter discussed in your document. Here, I'll provide a comprehensive glossary, including definitions and explanations for various terms that might be relevant to your content. Please note that the glossary terms can be customized based on the specific context of your document or topic.

Appendix B: Glossary

1.   **Algorithm**: A set of step-by-step instructions designed to solve a specific problem or perform a particular task. In the digital context, algorithms are often used in programming and data analysis.

2.   **Analytics**: The process of collecting, processing, and interpreting data to gain insights into trends, patterns, and user behavior. Analytics

tools are used to optimize strategies and decision-making.

3.   **Backlink**: A hyperlink on one website that directs users to another website. Backlinks are important for search engine optimization (SEO) as they can improve a site's authority and ranking in search results.

4.   **Content Management System (CMS)**: A software application or platform that enables users to create, manage, and publish digital content, such as websites and blogs.

5.   **Conversion Rate**: The percentage of users who take a desired action, such as making a purchase, signing up for a newsletter, or filling out a form.

6.   **Cybersecurity**: The practice of protecting digital systems, networks, and data from unauthorized access, attacks, and damage.

7.   **Domain Name**: A human-readable web address that represents the IP address of a website. For example, "www.example.com" is a domain name.

8.   **Engagement**: The level of interaction and participation that users have with digital content or platforms. Engagement can include likes, shares, comments, and other forms of user activity.

9. **Encryption:** To prevent unwanted access, data is transformed into a code. It is employed to protect the storage and transfer of data. **Hashtag:** A keyword or phrase preceded by the "#" symbol, used on social media platforms to categorize and organize content. Hashtags make it easier for users to find related posts.

10. **HTML (Hypertext Markup Language):** The standard language for creating web pages. HTML is used to structure and format the content on websites.

11. **Keyword:** A specific word or phrase used in digital content, especially in search engine optimization (SEO), to improve visibility in search engine results.

12. **Metadata:** Information about data, such as title, description, and tags, that provides context and enhances the discoverability of digital content.

13. **Responsive Design:** A web design approach that ensures a website adapts and displays correctly on various devices and screen sizes, such as smartphones, tablets, and desktops.

14. **Search Engine Optimization (SEO):** The process of optimizing digital content to improve its visibility in search engine results, thus increasing organic (non-paid) traffic.

15. **Social Media Marketing**: The use of social media platforms to promote products, services, or content. Social media marketing involves creating and sharing engaging content to reach and interact with a target audience.

16. **User Interface (UI)**: The visual and interactive elements of a digital platform that users interact with, including buttons, menus, and screens.

17. **User Experience (UX)**: The overall experience and satisfaction that a user has when interacting with a digital product or platform, including ease of use, accessibility, and visual design.

18. **Viral Marketing**: A marketing strategy that encourages users to share content with their network, leading to rapid and widespread dissemination.

19. **Webinar**: A live, online seminar or presentation that is conducted over the internet, allowing participants to interact and engage with the presenter.

20. **XML (eXtensible Markup Language)**: A versatile language used to define and structure data, often used for data interchange between systems and in web applications.

21. **2FA (Two-Factor Authentication)**: A security process that requires users to provide two different authentication factors to access an account, enhancing security by combining something the user knows

This glossary provides a reference for the key terms and concepts related to the digital realm and can help your audience better understand the content of your document. Customizing the glossary to align with your specific document's focus is recommended for clarity and relevance.

Thank you!

Thank you for your purchase. If you enjoyed this book, please kindly consider dropping us a review.